WHEN I FIND YOU AGAIN,
IT WILL BE IN MOUNTAINS

This book is dedicated to my father,
Tom O'Connor

WHEN I FIND YOU
AGAIN, IT WILL BE
IN MOUNTAINS

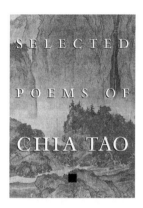

Translated from the Chinese

by MIKE O'CONNOR

WISDOM PUBLICATIONS • BOSTON

Wisdom Publications
199 Elm Street
Somerville, MA 02144 USA

Library of Congress Cataloging-in-Publication Data
Chia, Tao, 779-843.
    [Poems. English. Selections]
    When I find you again, it will be in mountains : selected poems
of Chia Tao / translated from the Chinese by Mike O'Connor.
        p. cm.
    Includes bibliographical references.
    ISBN 0-86171-172-6 (alk. paper)
    1. Chia, Tao, 779-843—Translations into English. I. O'Connor, Mike.
    II. Title.

    PL2677.C42 A26 2000
    895.1'13—dc21   00-043410

ISBN 0-86171-172-6

04   03   02   01
5   4   3   2

Cover and interior designed by Gopa and the Bear
Chinese Typesetting by TriStar Printing and Graphics
Cover image: Fan K'uan (fl. 990-1030), *Travelling among Mountains and Streams,*
                courtesy of the collection of the Palace Museum, Taiwan, Republic of
                China.
Interior images courtesy of Steven Johnson

Printed in Canada.

CONTENTS

Publisher's Acknowledgment

The publisher gratefully acknowledges the generous help of the Hershey Family Foundation in sponsoring the production of this book.

Publisher's Dedication

Wisdom Publications dedicates this work to Paul Miller, our friend and colleague. Here for too short a stay, may his presence continue to enrich us.

Acknowledgments

GRATEFUL ACKNOWLEDGMENT is made to the Pacific Cultural Foundation, Taipei, Taiwan, Republic of China, for a grant that helped to sustain research and translation for Book Two.

I thank both the Pacific Cultural Foundation and the Washington State Arts Commission (Olympia) for publication grants for my book *The Basin: Life in a Chinese Province* (Port Townsend: Empty Bowl Press, 1988), in which a number of these translations first appeared.

Shorter versions of the three books herein were first published in letterpress editions (Berkeley: Tangram, 1995, 1996, and 1998). My heartfelt thanks goes to Tangram publisher and printer Jerry Reddan, whose remarkable press nourishes a wide community of poets and poetry lovers.

Thanks are due *The Literary Review* (Fairleigh Dickinson University) and *Longhouse* (Vermont), where several of these translations first appeared.

I thank Steven Johnson, winter artist-in-residence at Centrum Foundation, Fort Worden, Port Townsend, for his two broadsides incorporating photographs of China and two poems of Chia Tao (Port Townsend: Kuan Yin/Empty Bowl Press, 2000).

A different version of Book One, *Colors of Daybreak and Dusk,* appeared in *The Clouds Should Know Me by Now: Buddhist Poet Monks of China,* edited by Red Pine and Mike O'Connor (Boston: Wisdom Publications, 1998).

Translator's Note

THE THREE BOOKS in this volume are versions of three limited-edition letterpress chapbooks previously published serially by Tangram. For this volume, I have added more poems to each of the books and expanded the notes and introduction. The arrangement of poems is intuitive rather than chronological. Each book is a story. Chronology was principally ruled out due to the fact that the eleven books, or *chuan,* of the poet, are not organized in chronological sequence, and because many of the poems cannot be accurately dated.

In my translations, I have chosen to make two lines in English for every one line in Chinese. I break the Chinese line because my own operating poetics tends to a short line. Also, when read in Chinese, the five-character line has a soft pause, or caesura, after the first two characters; in the seven-character line, there is a soft pause after the first two characters and another after the second two characters. To my own voice and ear, the division of the line in English seems natural.

With few exceptions, the style of romanization throughout the book is modified Wade-Giles.

I am deeply indebted to Chang Yu-ming for his master's thesis (National Taiwan Normal University, 1969), in which he provides almost all of the character variants of Chia Tao's texts. The work also identifies places and persons in the poems, and defines many difficult compounds and characters.

I am also deeply indebted to Catherine Witzling for her Ph.D. thesis on Chia Tao (Stanford University, 1980). Her excellent work has been an important source of reference for me since the mid-point of this undertaking, and is the only extensive study of Chia Tao in English to date. Her critical translations have also been a helpful cross-reference for a number of my own translations.

My indebtedness extends as well to Red Pine, who has insightfully gone through many of the poems with me, provided fresh historical and geographical information, and related firsthand accounts of travels in Buddhist-Taoist China.

I also want to express my gratitude to Burton Watson, whose translations and studies in the field of Chinese poetry and Ch'an Buddhism I have drawn on constantly.

In addition to the above, there are a number of people who have assisted me in this endeavor. I thank them all: Steven Johnson, Jack Estes, and Finn Wilcox for sharing, respectively, photographs, film footage, and poems from travels among China's hermits; Tim McNulty, who read many of these translations in manuscript and made astute suggestions; Bill Bridges, who made similar suggestions, including several important structural ones; Anselm Hollo, whose translation workshop at the Naropa Institute stimulated the formative phase of this project; Andrew Schelling, who encouraged this translation effort from its inception and offered criticism and good advice along the way; the Department of East Asian Languages and Civilizations at the University of Colorado, which granted me independent-scholar access to the Chinese materials of the department's library; Yen Hui-fei, who worked hard to improve my Mandarin; Hunter Golay, for tutoring me in Chinese grammar; Tim Casey, for tracking down invaluable Chinese materials; Wang Wei, who offered constructive criticism of my early translations; Lo Ch'ing, for the calligraphy in the Tangram books and for reading and talking about Chia Tao with me; Tim McNeill, Gene Smith, David Kittelstrom, Peter Bermudes, Wendy Cheng, and Samantha Kent at Wisdom Publications for their vision and hard work; and my wife, Liu Ling-hui, for just about everything else.

My inscriptions for the three books, as originally published, are:

Colors of Daybreak and Dusk
For Andrew Schelling & Anne Waldman

When the Tiger Hears the Sutra
To the Memory of Ivan Taylor, Printer (1903–1995)
and
For Jerry Reddan

One with the Snowy Night
For Niels Holm & Sitting Frog Zendo

Mike O'Connor
Morgan Hill
Port Townsend, Washington
February 2000
Year of the Dragon

Introduction

CHIA TAO (779–843) was a Ch'an (Zen) Buddhist monk until the age of thirty-one, when he took the extraordinary step of leaving the Buddhist order. His motives for this are not known, but his poems clearly reflect a life-long reverence for Buddhism. It is probable, however, that Chia Tao's decision had to do with his aspiration to devote himself more fully to the practice of poetry, a practice regarded by many at the time to be incompatible with formal religious life. It can be presumed that he also felt the need for a wider range of experience than monasticism afforded.

Chia Tao began his secular life in Ch'ang-an (modern-day Sian), the political and cultural capital of the T'ang Dynasty (618–906), where he was welcomed by prominent poets and became a member of a talented literary circle. He had less luck with political life, possibly serving in unspecified government positions in the capital and then, after suffering banishment late in life, in two minor provincial posts. He was always poor and often in bad health, but he stuck to the poetry.

Although Chia Tao put aside his monk's robe and bowl and lived most of his middle years in the capital, he never lost his deep affinity with the mountains and the "white clouds" of reclusion that he had known in his monastic training days. While a typical Chia Tao poem can be likened to a landscape picture consisting simply of a background of mountains and the presence of a figure at rest or traveling through, his poems altogether can be seen as a long horizontal scroll that, as it slowly unrolls, reveals sacred peaks; snow-bound hermit caves and temples; Ch'an masters and monks; Taoist immortals under pines; unending clouds; recluses in forest huts beside waterfalls or racing streams; pilgrims in tiny boats at sea or on canals; exiles on broad river plains, dusty roads, and at deserted inns; and nondescript sages in cloistered city abodes—from one end of China to the other. This "scroll" of miniature scenes and vast spaces quietly unfolds before us a world of highly unworldly human beings, whose spiritual work collectively brought forth a great religious age.

Chia Tao was born in Fan-yang (near today's Beijing) in 779. Twenty-four years earlier, the An Lu-shan rebellion had begun a warring and socially tumultuous period that all but ended one of the most culturally celebrated and economically prosperous reigns in the history of China. An Lu-shan, a powerful frontier commander, made war on the court and House of T'ang, and Emperor Hsuan-tsung (735–755), a generous patron of the arts, was ultimately forced by the rebels to abandon the capital at Ch'ang-an.

In 763, with a change in fortune resulting in the overthrow of An Lu-shan, who was murdered in a plot instigated by his son, a nominal restoration of T'ang power was brought about. But though the dynasty would continue for more than a hundred years, it was never able to reassert control over a number of resource-rich provinces.

The post-rebellion T'ang reign was also mired in financial problems and unable to match the cultural opulence of Emperor Hsuan-tsung's reign. In the opinion of historians, the turmoil of the rebellion and its strained aftermath—at times resembling conditions in China's period of feudal warlords—created a discontinuity between the celebrated culture of the High T'ang and that of the Middle and Late T'ang.

The period brought great suffering to millions of people, costing a staggering number of lives, and costing others their homes or their way of life. The turmoil did not spare China's greatest poets. Li Po (701–762), for instance, became ensnared in one of the many intrigues to establish an administration at Nanking. He subsequently defected, but was nonetheless arrested and jailed for several months before being sent into exile in Chiang-nan, that miasmic land south of the Yangtze River. Tu Fu (712–770) persisted for some time in seeking a position in the capital, but after failing repeatedly, retired to Cheng-tu in Szechuan. He died with his heart still set on returning to Ch'ang-an, his home and the center of poetry. Finally, the great painter and poet Wang Wei (700–761) was nearly executed for treason.

Chia Tao came of age as the end of the eighth century drew near. Though the empire was still struggling to right itself, it was a comparatively peaceful time and one in which Buddhism—especially Ch'an Buddhism—was flourishing. Like poetry in many historical respects, Buddhism in China also reached an apogee around the time of Hsuan-tsung's reign. This golden age of Buddhism was highlighted by the flowering of Ch'an, a convergence of Buddhism and Taoism that had been developing for the several centuries since the arrival from India of Bodhidharma in the late fifth century.

As Heinrich Dumoulin describes it in *Zen Buddhism: A History,*

> The Chinese Zen Buddhist movement during the T'ang period can be reckoned among the most amazing phenomena in the history of religions. The mixing of Buddhist and Taoist elements resulted in a contribution to religious history that was both unique and enriching.... The adaptation of Indian Buddhist teachings to the Chinese character was fully achieved; Indian metaphysics melded with Chinese ways of thinking and adapted to Chinese linguistic patterns.

Exactly when or why Chia Tao became a monk is not known. No details about his family exist, though most historians believe the family was poor. All that is clear is that he left home and traveled to the eastern capital of Loyang, where he embarked on Buddhist monastic life under the religious name of Wu-pen. Sometime later, he took up residence in the Blue Dragon Monastery in Ch'ang-an, the largest and most populous city in the world at the time.

Because there is no biographical record of his monastic life, Chia Tao virtually disappears from view for at least a decade. A few of his poems do mention his temple days, but none are identified as having been written while he was a monk. His official biography notes, however, that in Lo-yang, he wrote a poem protesting a curfew that forbade monks to go out after noon. The poem caught the sympathetic eye of the eminent Confucian poet Han Yu (768–824), who later became one of Chia Tao's principal poetry mentors.

A more famous account—a literary anecdote—describes the meeting of the poets this way: Chia Tao, while riding a donkey to the marketplace, was deeply absorbed in trying to choose between two words, "push" *(t'ui)* and "knock" *(ch'iao)* in the line: "In moonlight, a monk [knocks at, or pushes] a gate." Reciting the line over and over, Chia Tao was oblivious of his surroundings and collided with a sedan chair carrying Han Yu, then the metropolitan governor of the capital. Han Yu, waving off Chia Tao's apologies, became interested in his poetic impasse, and immediately opted for the word "knock." The compound "push-knock" *(t'ui-ch'iao)* became thereafter the traditional term to describe not only Chia Tao's assiduousness of craft, but any poet's exacting labor to find the *mot juste* or make careful stylistic distinctions. (The incident was also used to criticize Chia Tao for deviating from the poetics of direct experience and realism to move in the direction of poetic stylization, something other craft-conscious poets of the mid-T'ang would begin to do with good effect.)

Scholars have noted that the story is certainly apocryphal (Han Yu was living away from the capital at the time alleged), but both stories support other evidence that Han Yu—the leading figure of a literary circle that advocated a "restoration of antiquity" *(fu-ku)*—may have influenced Chia Tao's decision to leave the Buddhist order. Whatever the case, a close literary friendship did develop between the Confucian and the former Buddhist monk.

When Chia Tao settled into life in Ch'ang-an, the cultural milieu of the capital was still fertile ground for poetry. From the number of poems either dedicated to or written about him, and from the large number of poems he wrote about or dedicated to others, it is evident that Chia Tao had many literary and scholarly friends.

He was particularly drawn to the poets Ch'ang Chi (c. 776–c. 829), Meng Chiao (751–814), and Han Yu, who would become his teachers; and to the poets Wang Chien (c. 751–c. 830), Yao Ho (fl. 831), and Li P'en (dates uncertain), who would become his close friends. It has been said of Chia Tao that his deepest quest was for poetic mastery and, related to this, to finding *chih-yin,* people who understood and appreciated his poetry—a time-honored endeavor in Chinese literary history. Chia Tao had the good fortune to live in a time when poets were highly supportive and appreciative of one another.

From accounts by his contemporaries, Chia Tao was a handsome and gravely elegant man, tall and probably thin. Sometime while living in Ch'ang-an he married a woman surnamed Liu, but she is never mentioned in his poems; in that age of poetry, it was uncommon for a poet to write about his wife, or about domestic life in general. All that is known about the couple is that they apparently did not have children and that she handled his funeral arrangements.

One of the most important persons Chia Tao became acquainted with in Ch'ang-an was the highly respected poet Meng Chiao, whom he first met in 812. Later, the famed Sung Dynasty poet Su Tung-po (1037–1101), reflecting on Meng Chiao, said that his every poem came from his heart and marrow—passionate, sincere, and more than a little bitter. Su Tung-po also began one of his two poems on Meng Chiao's poetry with the line, "I can't stand the poems of Meng Chiao."

Meng Chiao, twenty-eight years Chia Tao's senior, proved a strong influence on the younger poet. A child during the An Lushan Rebellion, Meng Chiao suffered terribly in its aftermath. In his youth, he spent a number of years as a recluse on Sung-shan Mountain; later, he traveled extensively in the south. He failed the imperial examination *(chin-shih)* twice, passing it only in his fortieth year. Together with Chia Tao and Li Ho (791–817), he was a member of Han Yu's circle of poets and, for a while, worked closely with Han Yu in experimental poetics.

Chia Tao, Li Ho, and Meng Chiao were later also grouped togeth-er in a school of poetry called Ku-yin shih-ren (literally, "bitter-singing poets"). Lack of material and political success and other hardships haunt their poetry: Li Ho died in broken health at age twenty-six, and Meng Chiao's sons died in infancy. Meng Chiao and Chia Tao's poems were described, respectively, as *han* (cold and tough) and *shou* (lean or thin). It is said that Meng Chiao, upon first encountering the tall imposing figure of the younger poet, called him "a lean monk lying in ice"—this from an old poet who him-self was a poverty-saddled recluse! Their poetry was distinct from mainstream literature, represented at the time by the work of Po Chu-i (772–846), and court poetry.

When Meng Chiao died, it is recorded that dark clouds hung over the capital for days, and the mourning was so deep and per-vasive that the nation's poets were unable to write any new poems. Many felt that no more poetry could be written during the dynasty. But then Chia Tao came forward and penned an elegy for Meng Chiao, and the great cloud of grief lifted, and poetry once again flowed in T'ang China. Han Yu declared that Chia Tao must have arrived on the scene providentially to take up the fallen mantel of Meng Chiao.

Chia Tao sat for the imperial examination (monasteries, among other things, served as environments for preparing monks for the exam), but whether he actually passed the exam isn't clear, though he seems to have taken it more than once. Scholars point out that poets of the T'ang sought civil service positions with utmost seri-ousness, but Chia Tao's interest in politics was always weak and his attempt to secure government employment lacked appropriate vig-or. Certainly, Chia Tao's sensibility was an odd fit for the bureau-cracy (as were Meng Chiao's and Li Ho's, for that matter), but con-cerns over finances kept him in the hunt.

Except for occasional excursions and retreats, Chia Tao did not stray far from Ch'ang-an in his middle years. He wrote a number of poems describing persons and scenes in the city, especially with-in the Sheng-tao ward, in the southeast corner of Ch'ang-an near

Serpentine Lake, where he moved in 826. Through the years in Ch'ang-an, however, Chia Tao maintained his old ties with the eremites in China's mountains and remote temples. As a poet and former monk, Chia Tao clearly had the credentials to come and go freely in the white clouds. He was attuned to what was happening in the mountains and other places of contemplative retreat. Though his poems reveal that he chided himself for not being more deeply realized, it may be that his sense of limitation in this regard only enhanced his admiration of those who were.

The Chung-nan Mountains are the divide of north and south China and stretch to the Chi-lien Mountains to the west, which in turn become the Kunlun Mountains extending to the border of northern India. In ancient times, this cordillera was called Chung-nan-shan and harbored China's shamans-turned-hermits, who took refuge in the mountains after losing their power to newly civilizing elements. Bill Porter notes in *Road to Heaven,*

> Hermits were shamans and diviners, herbalists and doctors, adepts at the occult and the manifest. Their world was far bigger than the walled-in world of the city. Detached from values imposed by whim or custom, hermits have remained an integral part of Chinese society because of the commitment to their culture's own most ancient values. If nothing else, they represent its mythic past, and that past is nowhere more apparent than in [the Chung-nan Mountains].

It was this magical religious shamanism and hermeticism that evolved into Taoism, which in the first through third centuries A.D. served as a hospitable environment for the wave of Buddhist pilgrims that came to China from India. These combining influences spawned Ch'an Buddhism, which reached its full maturity in the eighth and ninth centuries.

In Chia Tao's time, the mountains of China held sages who might be of any one, two, or three of the seven or eight Buddhist schools, and of any number of Taoist sects as well. Even Confucians had established by then a tradition of mountain retreat. In Chia Tao's middle-to-late years, his religious and philosophical orientation deepened. He became increasingly like Li Po, a man of *chu-shih* (leaving the world), a *fo/lao-ren*, (Buddha/Tao man); in contrast, Tu Fu, not unlike Han Yu, is traditionally seen as a man of *ru-shih* (entering into the world), or of Confucianism. Chia Tao's poems give meaning to the life of the *chu-shih* man and provide scrupulous witness to the period's wilderness-sage tradition.

Late in life (837), Chia Tao was denounced, apparently unfairly, and banished to a provincial post: Registry Clerk of Ch'ang Chiang County in Szechuan Province. This, curiously, was his first position of official record. In 840, he was promoted to Granary Administrator of P'u-chou (in today's Sui-ning County). Three years later, he was appointed Administrator of Finances for the same district, but he died before assuming the office. Based on his service in Ch'ang-chiang, the county name became one of his literary names.

Chia Tao died during the reign of Wu-tsung in 843, when the empire under the house of T'ang was at its highest point since the An Lu-shan debacle, and just before its final downward spiral. The previous year had seen the beginning of a period of Buddhist persecution that would last three years and include confiscation of many Buddhist landholdings, and widespread destruction of temples and shrines. A revival of Confucianism and a desire to curb the accumulation of property owned by Buddhist temples were in part responsible for the suppression. Afterward, however, Buddhism rebounded sufficiently to continue having a strong influence; this was true especially of Ch'an Buddhism.

Chia Tao died in humble circumstances: without money and with only two known possessions—a donkey in bad health and a five-string zither. He was survived by his wife, but no children. Still, Chia Tao never anticipated worldly rewards. He attained a high degree of poetic excellence that has earned him grateful readers up to the present—whether it be the school children in Taiwan reciting his most famous poems or the modern underground Misty poets of mainland China gleaning elements from his work for use in their linguistically ambiguous experimental poetics.

While Chia Tao's exercising principle was poetry, his religious practice was inseparable from his art. He was, in Shunryu Suzuki's words describing American Zen students, "not priest, not exactly laymen." This ambiguous status, while perhaps posing questions of identity for Chia Tao, contributed to his unique range of access to mountain sages and to Ch'ang-an literati alike. Lang-hsien, or "Wandering Immortal," the literary name given to him by his peers, does honor to the poet and the pilgrim, whose work has already lived 1,200 years.

Notes on the Poetry

Chia Tao's early poetry has been classified as in the *fu-ku* (return to antiquity) mode advanced in Han Yu's literary circle. The poetics of this style emphasized traditional values and tended to be discursive and moralistic. On the other hand, experimentation of style and diction was encouraged, particularly as Chia Tao did, in efforts to consciously make poetry less "beautiful"—hopefully, thereby, making it more significant and true. Catherine Witzling, in her Ph.D. thesis on Chia Tao, states that the poet in this early phase "elevated clumsiness to the status of a poetic goal." This purposeful avoidance of high style and polished technique is not an unusual strategy for young poets anywhere as a reaction to earlier highly cultivated or canonical poetry.

As Chia Tao matured, his style changed; he began to incorporate the quietism and spirit associated with Buddhism and Taoism. This style, which remained fairly constant through the years, gives us those quintessential Chia Tao poems describing austere temple settings or lichen-dotted hermit caves. Atmosphere or mood, in many instances, is the most expressive or tangible element of the poem. At their purest, these lyrics might be compared to the cold stone chimes sounded at temples to gently summon monks out of deep meditation or trance. Their sonority is subtle and elusive.

The undercurrent of sadness that flows through Chia Tao's work—the Ku-yin shih-ren strain—was surely fed by his chronic poverty and inconsequential political status; but it rarely gives way in his mature work to bitterness, self-pity or pessimism (despite Su Teng-p'o's opinion to the contrary). The formula for the middle-late Chia Tao poem, according to Chinese literary critics, is *kau-hsin* (lofty and heartfelt), yet simultaneously *p'ing-tan* (ordinary and plain). It is this "ordinary and plain" quality of his verse, imbued with a sense of emotional detachment, that has contributed to Chia Tao's being somewhat underappreciated. Chia Tao, like *p'u-erh* (scholar's tea), is an acquired taste. And ultimately, he made the p'ing-tan poem great.

Chia Tao wrote in both old-style ku-shih and modern-style *lu-shih* (regulated) verse forms, but it was the latter at which he was to become most accomplished and influential. The former consists of poems of no set length with lines of either five or seven characters. It was a poetic form suited for longer narrative content that yielded some of his best fu-ku poems.

The lu-shih consists of eight lines of either five or seven characters each. This verse form also required certain end-rhymes and complex tonal arrangements, as well as a scheme of parallel lines for at least two of the four couplets. Each line is usually end-stopped; enjambment is uncommon. The lu-shih form was first effectively used with serious themes by Tu Fu, who in turn influenced Meng Chiao's late poems. Chia Tao built on both poets' work. His compressed and carefully wrought lu-shih poems gained him many disciples, even spawning whole schools of poetry, in the Late T'ang and beyond. In these poems, Chia Tao is praised for what came to be called his "inner nature-couplets," in which similar or contrasting nature imagery is juxtaposed in parallel lines. The couplets share much in common with the later Japanese haiku form as well as the modern imagist poem.

Chia Tao's extant poems number 404. The farewell poem is most widely represented, accounting for nearly one hundred. As scholars have pointed out, poems of parting resonated deeply with Chinese of the T'ang era because of the huge distances within China, primitive transportation, and the strong ties of friendship and family. For Chia Tao, a poem on the theme of farewell was ritualistic, a gift to the traveler as well as a means for the poet to ease his own depression or sadness at separation. In these poems, Chia Tao demonstrates a remarkable empathy with other men.

In addition to the farewell poem, Chia Tao follows in the footsteps of earlier T'ang poets by choosing to write about visits to mountain sages, overnight stays at monasteries, and meetings with hermits. But unlike his predecessors, Chia Tao made these poems the core of his work. (As for the poetry of reclusion in general, it dates back at least as far as T'ao Yuan-ming (365–427).)

Like the poems of the emerging Buddhist poet-monks—another circle with which Chia Tao had close contact—Chia Tao's poems are filled with imagery of temples and stone chimes, looming peaks, wind-twisted pines, stone pagodas, and monks in meditation, but there are few doctrinal poems. Buddhism is largely internalized; the expression of Buddhist ideas is aesthetic, not philosophical. Chia Tao's years of training as a monk likely had something to do with his artistic temperament—he composed poems that are spare, technically hard-won *(t'ui-ch'iao)* and morally serious—and his choice of religious subject matter. Overall, though, his poems are in a literary and secular vein.

The earnestness and sincerity of Chia Tao's attitude toward poetry is suggested by an anecdote: Each New Year's eve he would gather together all of the poems he had written in the year, place them on a table in his home before a small altar and sprinkle them with wine, saying to the gods, "Here is my heart's blood for one year." The offering made, the Wandering Immortal would then drink up the rest of the wine and sing.

Colors of
Daybreak and Dusk

B O O K   O N E

策杖馳山驛逢人問梓州長江那可到行客替生愁

寄令狐相公

SENT TO MINISTER LING-HU

With walking stick, he hurries
from post to mountain post,

asking everyone he meets
how far it is to Tzu-chou.

But Ch'ang-chiang's,
in fact, too far by foot;

and travelers,
feeling for him, all feel for him.

WINTER NIGHT FAREWELL

At first light, you ride
swiftly over the village bridge;

plum blossoms fall
on the stream and unmelted snow.

With the days short and the weather cold,
it's sad to see a guest depart;

the Ch'u Mountains go on and on,
and the road...

冬夜送人

平明走馬上村橋花落梅溪雪未消

日短天寒愁送客楚山無限路迢迢

二月晦日留別鄴中友人

立馬柳花裏別君當酒酣春風漸向北雲鴈不飛南

明曉日初一今年月又三鞭羸去暮色遠岳起煙嵐

MEMENTO ON THE DEPARTURE
OF A FRIEND FROM YEH,
LAST DAY OF THE SECOND MOON

In flowering willows,
we rein in our horses;
at parting, we are free
to drink all the wine we desire.

But the winds of spring
sweep slowly north;
clouds and wild geese
do not fly south.

Tomorrow
dawns the first—
already the third
month of the year!

Touch whip to lean horse and go
into the colors of dusk;
mist is rising
on far peaks.

MORNING TRAVEL

Rising early
to begin the journey;
not a sound
from the chickens next door.

Beneath the lamp,
I part from the innkeeper;
on the road, my skinny horse
moves through the dark.

Slipping on stones
newly frosted,
threading through woods,
we scare up birds roosting.

After a bell sounds
far in the mountains,
the colors of daybreak
gradually form.

早行

早起赴前程鄰雞尚未鳴主人燈下別羸馬暗中行

蹋石新霜滑穿林宿鳥驚遠山鐘動後曙色漸分明

暮過山村

數里聞寒水山家少四鄰怪禽啼曠野落日恐行人

初月未終夕邊烽不過秦蕭條桑柘外煙火漸相親

PASSING BY A MOUNTAIN VILLAGE AT DUSK

For several *li*
I've been hearing the cold stream;
but at these mountain homes,
there's no one about.

Strange birds
cry in the wilds;
the sun going down
unsettles the traveler.

A new moon shines,
but won't last the evening;
border signal towers
do not reach past Ch'in.

Beyond the deserted grove
of mulberry and *chih*—
cook smoke,
coming closer.

OVERNIGHT AT A MOUNTAIN MONASTERY

Massed peaks pierce
the sky's cold colors;
here, the trail junctions
with the temple path.

Shooting stars pass
into sparse-branched trees;
the moon travels one way,
clouds the other.

Few people come
to this mountaintop;
cranes do not flock
in the tall pines.

One Buddhist monk,
eighty years old,
has never heard
of the world's affairs.

宿山寺

眾岫聳寒色精廬向此分
流星透疏木走月逆行雲
絕頂人來少高松鶴不群
一僧年八十世事未曾聞

送知
興上
人

久
住
巴
興
寺
如
今
始
拂
衣
欲
臨
秋
水
別
不
向
故
園
歸

錫
挂
天
涯
樹
房
開
嶽
頂
扉
下
看
萬
里
曉
霜
海
日
生
微

FAREWELL TO MONK CHIH-HSING

You have lived a long time
at Pa-hsing Temple;
retired, you're preparing
only now to leave.

On the verge of parting, we look
out upon bright autumn water;
you're not returning to your hometown,
nor to the country around it.

You will hang your Buddhist staff in a tree
where the sky reaches to a watery horizon;
where the door-leaf of your hut
opens on great mountains.

Below, you will see dawn
a thousand *li* away:
a miniature sun
born of a cold white sea.

WATCHING THE LATE DAY CLEAR
AFTER SNOWFALL

Leaning on my staff,
I watch the sky clearing after snow:
layer upon layer
of mountains, streams and mist.

A woodcutter
returns to his cottage,
as the cold sun sets
on perilous peaks.

A farmer's fire
burns grass along a ridge;
wisps of cook smoke float
in rock-girt pines.

Returning to the temple
along the mountain road,
I hear the striking
of the evening bell.

雪晴晚望

倚杖望晴雪
溪雲幾萬重
樵人歸白屋
寒日下危峰
野火燒岡草
斷煙生石松
卻迴山寺路
聞打暮天鐘

易州登龍興寺樓望郡北高峰

郡北最高峰巉巖絕雲路朝來上樓望稍覺得幽趣

朦朧碧煙裏群嶺若相附何時一登陟萬物皆下顧

AT I-CHOU, CLIMBING THE TOWER
OF LUNG-HSING TEMPLE
TO VIEW THE HIGH NORTHERN MOUNTAINS

The tallest peaks
north of the district—
cliffs so high
the road is lost in clouds.

At dawn,
I climb the tower for a look,
gradually feeling
their serene effect.

In smoke-blue
haze,
massed peaks
appear as if joined.

When will I climb
and set foot there,
and gaze on all
creation below?

SEEKING BUT NOT FINDING THE RECLUSE

Under pines
I ask the boy;

he says: "My master's gone
to gather herbs.

I only know
he's on this mountain,

but the clouds are too deep
to know where."

尋隱者不遇
松下問童子言師採藥去只在此山中雲深不知處

題隱者居

雖有柴門長不關片雲孤木伴身閒猶嫌住久人知處

見擬移家更上山

WRITTEN AT THE DWELLING OF A RECLUSE

Even though you have a brushwood door,
it hasn't been shut for a long time;

a few clouds, a few trees
have been your only companions.

Still, I suspect if you stay longer,
people will learn of this spot;

we'll see you moving
higher on the mountain.

ABODE OF THE UNPLANNED EFFECT

The grass-covered path
is secluded and still;
a closed door faces
the Chung-nan Mountains.

In the evening, the air's chilly,
but the light rain stops;
at dawn, far off,
a few cicadas start.

Leaves fall
where no green earth remains;
a person at his ease
wears a common white robe.

With simplicity and plainness
his original nature still,
what need to practice
calming of the heart?

芫齋

草合徑微微　終南對掩扉
晚涼疏雨絕　初曉遠蟬稀
落葉無青地　閒身著白衣
朴愚猶本性　不是學忘機

送田卓入華山

幽深足暮蟬驚覺石床眠瀑布五千仞草堂瀑布邊

壇松涓滴露嶽月沉寥天鶴過君須看上頭應有仙

A FAREWELL TO T'IEN CHO
ON RETREAT ON HUA MOUNTAIN

Deep and hidden, cicadas
fill the dusk;
startled, you awaken
from a stone bed.

Near your hut,
a waterfall
falls
thousands of feet.

Pines near the altar
drip dew;
the mountain moon
shines in vast clear space.

When a crane passes over,
you must see—
it should bear
an immortal.

MENG JUNG, GAINFULLY UNEMPLOYED

Your residence, Meng,
overlooks the river;
but you do not eat
the fish in it.

Your brown robe
is sewn of coarse cloth;
only silk-bound books
fill your bamboo shelves.

The solitary bird
loves the wood;
your heart is also
not of the world.

You plan to row away
in a lone boat, and
build another hut—
in which mountains?

孟融逸人

孟君臨水居不食水中魚
衣褐唯麤帛篋箱秖素書
樹林幽鳥戀世界此心疏
擬棹孤舟去何峰又結廬

旅遊

此心非一事書札若為傳
舊國別多日故人無少年
空巢霜葉落疏牖水螢穿
留得林僧宿中宵坐默然

WHILE TRAVELING

With so much on my mind,
it's hard to express myself in letters.

How long is it since I left home?
Old friends are no longer young.

Frosted leaves fall into empty bird nests;
river fireflies weave through open windows.

I stop at a forest monk's
and spend the night in quiet sitting.

SEEING OFF SUB-PREFECT MU TO MEI-CHOU

Sword Gate leans
by the clear Han River;
you have never passed
this way before.

From dawn to dusk,
the travelers are few;
deep in mountains,
many birds are unfamiliar.

The cry of gibbons
joins rain in the gorges;
the planked road along cliffs
ends at river waves.

One road
in white clouds,
where flying streams
splash climbing vines.

送穆少府知眉州
劍門倚清漢君昔未曾過日暮行人少山深異鳥多
猿啼和峽雨棧盡到江波一路白雲裏飛泉灑薜蘿

宿村家亭子

床頭枕是溪中石
井底泉通竹下池
宿客未眠過夜半
獨聞山雨到來時

SPENDING THE NIGHT
AT A VILLAGER'S PAVILION

The pillow for his bed
is a rock from mid-stream;

the spring from the well-bottom
flows to a pond through bamboo.

The night is half gone,
but the guest hasn't slept;

he alone hears
the mountain rain arrive.

OVERNIGHT IN CH'ENG-HSIANG FOREST

We're visiting together
when the sun goes down,
in a forest of a thousand trees
not yet bare of leaves.

A rock-tangled creek
flows out the valley;
mountain rain
drips on a perching owl.

Around our lamp,
we hear the water clock flow;
thanks to the host,
the guest stays up late.

We enjoyed
this evening fully;
but…ah,
if the moon had shone.

宿成湘林下
相訪夕陽時千株木未衰石泉流出谷山雨滴栖鷗
漏向燈聽數君因客寢遲今宵不盡興更有月明期

送丹師歸閩中

波濤路杳然衰柳洛陽蟬
歸林久別寺過越未離船
行李經雷電禪前漱島泉
自說從今去身應老海邊

FAREWELL TO MASTER TAN
RETURNING TO MIN

From Lo-yang's autumn willows
and cicadas,
your route is a lonely one
of whitecap and wave.

Your belongings will pass
through thunder and lightning;
at a spring on an island
you'll bathe before sitting.

After long absence,
you're returning to your temple in the trees,
not putting ashore,
as you sail the coast of Yueh.

You say today is set
for your departure,
that you expect to grow old
by the sea.

AT NI-YANG INN

A traveler's sadness,
how is it deepened?
By seeing off
an old friend at dusk.

At the run-down inn,
autumn fireflies are gone;
in the empty town,
a winter rain is coming.

The sun sets
in shimmering white dew;
tree shadows sweep
the green moss.

As I sit alone,
my mood after parting darkens;
the light of my single lamp
is weak.

泥陽館

客愁何併起暮送故人回
廢館秋螢出空城寒雨來
夕陽飄白露樹影掃青苔
獨坐離容慘孤燈照不開

33

送友人如邊

去日重陽後前程菊正芳行車輾秋岳落葉墜寒霜

雲入漢天白風高磧色黃蒲輪待恐晚求薦向諸方

FAREWELL TO A FRIEND LEAVING
FOR THE FRONTIER

You depart
after Double Nine,
at the time of full
chrysanthemum fragrance.

In autumn mountains,
carriages are easily overturned;
fallen leaves decay
in the frosted earth.

Clouds appear
in the white Han River sky;
high winds blow
across reaches of yellow sand.

You fear it's too late
to wrap the wheels for safety,
go searching in all directions
for food and a place to stay.

憶江上吳處士
閩國揚帆去蟾蜍虧復圓秋風生渭水落葉滿長安
此地聚會夕當時雷雨寒蘭橈殊未返消息海雲端

THINKING OF RETIRED SCHOLAR WU
ON THE RIVER

Since you set sail
for the state of Min,
the moon has passed
from full to full again.

Autumn wind
arises on Wei River;
falling leaves
fill Ch'ang-an.

I recall
that evening together—
suddenly thunder,
then cold rain…

Odd your orchidwood oar
hasn't yet returned;
news of you ends
at ocean clouds.

HAPPY THAT OFFICIAL YAO IS RETURNING FROM HANG-CHOU

Along the route,
grove after grove of maples;
each day
you anchor in their cool shade.

Coming and going,
adrift on the flowing water—
haste would have been more suited
to my heart.

You write one poem
on the river;
chant it three times
in moonlight.

At the Hall of Government Affairs,
you'll assume a post of high rank;
I regret not looking for you
at Cloud Gate.

喜姚郎中自杭州迴

路多楓樹林累日泊清陰
來去泛流水翛然適此心
一披江上作三起月中吟
東省期司諫雲門悔不尋

江亭晚望

浩渺浸雲根煙嵐沒遠村
鳥歸沙有跡帆過浪無痕
望水知柔性看山欲倦魂
縱情猶未已迴馬欲黃昏

LATE IN THE DAY, GAZING OUT
FROM A RIVER PAVILION

Water to the horizon
veils the base of clouds;
mountain mist
blurs a far village.

Returning to nest,
birds make tracks in the sand;
passing on the river,
a boat leaves no trace on the waves.

I gaze at the water
and know its gentle nature;
watch the mountains
until my spirit tires.

Though not yet ready
to leave off musing,
dusk falls,
and I return by horse.

AUSPICIOUS ARRIVAL OF YUNG T'AO

This morning
laughing together—
just a few such days
in a hundred.

After birds pass
over Sword Gate, it's calm;
invaders from the south
have withdrawn to the Lu River wilds.

We walk on frosted ground
praising chrysanthemums bordering fields;
sit on the east edge of the woods
waiting for the moon to rise.

Not having to be alone
is happiness;
we do not talk
of failure or success.

喜雍陶至

今朝笑語同幾日
百憂中鳥度劍門靜
蠻歸瀘水空

步霜吟菊畔待月
坐林東且莫孤
此興勿論窮與通

39

送于總持歸京

出家初隸何方寺上國西明御水東
別來二十一春風御見舊房皆下樹

SEEING OFF THE MONK TS'UNG-CH'IH
RETURNING TO THE CAPITAL

"When you left home
to be a monk,
to which temple
did you first go?"

"Ch'ang-an's
Western Light,
east of the waters
of the palace canal.

Going back, I'll see again
the ancient buildings
and, below the steps,
the trees,

which, since I left,
have known
twenty-one
winds of spring."

RESPONSE TO SUB-PREFECT LI K'UO
OF HU COUNTY

I can't help feeling for you—
leaving your office work
only to meet each time
the dying day.

On northern slopes,
frost stiffens bamboo;
on South Mountain,
streams flow to bamboo fences.

I sigh,
thinking of my blue-sea companion;
but it's useless
to entreat a white-cloud master.

Regretfully,
we can't set out together;
only a wild crane
knows my heart.

吟懷滄海侶空問白雲師恨不相從去心惟野鶴知

稍憐公事退復遇夕陽時北朔霜凝竹南山水入籬

訓鄂縣李廓少府見寄

41

宿懸泉驛

曉行瀝水樓暮到懸泉驛林月值雲遮山燈照愁寂

OVERNIGHT AT HSUAN-CH'UAN
COURIER STATION

Early morning,
leave from Li-shui Tower;

by dusk arrive
at Hsuan-ch'uan station.

Just when clouds cover
the forest moon,

a mountain lamp
shines in the desolate calm.

SPRING TRAVEL

Keeping on and on,
a traveler gets farther, farther away;
dust without cease
follows a horse through the world.

A traveler's feelings
once the sun's rays slant—
spring colors
in the morning mist.

The river's flow heard
at the empty inn—
courtesans stirring
at the old palace.

I think of home
a thousand *li* away;
green willow wind
stirs on the pond.

春行

去去行人遠塵隨馬不窮旅情斜日後春色早煙中
流水穿空館閒花發故宮舊鄉千里思池上綠楊風

The Tiger
Hears the Sutra

B O O K   T W O

渡桑乾

客舍幷州已十霜

歸心日夜憶咸陽

無端更渡桑乾水

卻望幷州是故鄉

FERRYING ACROSS THE DRY MULBERRY RIVER

A newcomer to P'ing-chou,
he stayed there ten years;
day and night
missing his old home, Ch'ang-an.

Then, inexplicably,
he went farther, across the Dry Mulberry;
only to look back on P'ing-chou
as home.

TAKING LEAVE OF A BUDDHIST MASTER,
DEPARTING CHINA

In Yueh,
at which temple will you stay?
From the southeast,
your return must be by water.

On the autumn Yangtze,
you wash one rice bowl
for every third robe
dried in the sun.

In silence, hear
the cries of long-traveled swans;
on the move, see
leaves flying in the shade.

In your bag,
you have nothing of value;
at night, the boat's crew
seldom bolts the doors.

送去華法師

在越局何寺東南水路歸秋江洗一缽寒日曬三衣

默聽鴻聲盡行看葉影飛囊中無寶貨船戶夜局稀

47

柳絮落濛濛西州道路中相逢春忽盡獨去講初終
行疾遙山雨眠遲後夜風遠房三兩樹迴去葉應紅
送神邈法師

SEEING OFF SHEN-MIAO, BUDDHIST MASTER

Mists of willow catkin
are falling
on the roads
of western Szechuan.

We meet—
then suddenly spring is over;
your teachings imparted,
you go alone,

traveling fast on seeing
rain in far mountains;
sleeping late after
a storm in the night.

When you return,
the leaves on the trees
around your hermitage
should be vermilion.

SEEING OFF A MAN OF THE TAO

When I find you again,
it will be in mountains;
this morning, I lose you
once more to farewell.

Free of attachment
in heart and mind—
is it why you can go
ten thousand *li* alone

to places with such
little human warmth,
where, when you meet someone,
they speak an ancient tongue?

Traveling without disciples,
you have only
a white dog
for company.

送道者
獨向山中見今朝又別離一心無挂住萬里獨何之
到處絕煙火逢人說古時此行無弟子白犬自相隨

寄無可上人
僻寺多高樹涼天憶重遊磬過溝水盡月入草堂秋
穴蟻苔痕靜藏蟬柏葉稠名山思徧往早晚到嵩丘

SENT TO A HUA MOUNTAIN MONK

From afar,
I know your white-rock hermitage,
hidden in a haze
of evergreen trees.

When the moon sets,
it's mind-watching time;
clouds arise
in your closed eyes.

Just before dawn, temple bells
sound from neighboring peaks;
waterfalls hang thousands of feet
in emptiness.

Moss and lichen
cover the cliff face;
a narrow, indistinct path
leads to you.

FOR A BUDDHIST MONK

In a tangle of mountains,
in autumn trees, a cave—
hidden within,
a magic dragon pearl.

Poplar and cassia
overlook a blue sea;
rare fragrances waft
from a stone pagoda.

A monk since youth,
you still have no white hair;
you enter upon meditation,
in a frost-streaked robe.

Here there is no talk
of the world's affairs—
those matters that make
wild the hearts of men.

贈僧

亂山秋木穴裏有靈蛇藏楊桂臨滄海石樓聞異香

出塵頭未白入定衲凝霜莫話五湖事令人心欲狂

送僧遊衡嶽

心知衡嶽路不怕去人稀船裏猶鳴磬溪頭自曝衣

有家從小別無寺不言歸料得逢寒往當禪雪滿扉

SEEING OFF A BUDDHIST MONK
TRAVELING TO HENG MOUNTAIN

Your heart knows
the way to Heng Mountain;
you are not afraid
few people go there.

Inside the boat,
you still hear birds and temple chimes;
at the river's source,
you dry your monk's robe in the sun.

You had a family,
but left it when young;
now there is no temple
that would not welcome you.

Managing to find
a shelter in the cold,
you do your usual zazen
as snow fills up your door.

SENT TO MONKS CHEN AND K'UNG
AT LUNG-CH'IH TEMPLE

You both were called
to stay in the Chung-nan Mountains;
now you can't take leave
of Stone Bridge.

In the forest,
signs of autumn cease;
on the high peak,
night meditation lasts long.

Cold grass and mist
hide tigers;
the moon
lights a hawk in tall pines.

I'll arrive at the temple
in the time of frosty skies—
that temple built
dynasties ago.

寄龍池寺貞空二上人
龍池寺貞空二上人
受請終南住俱妙去石橋林中秋信絕峰頂夜禪遙
寒草煙藏虎高松月照鶻霜天期到寺寺置即前朝

哭柏巖禪師

苔覆石床新師曾占幾春寫留行道影焚卻坐禪身

塔院關松雪經房鎖隙塵自嫌雙淚下不是解空人

MOURNING THE DEATH
OF CH'AN MASTER PO-YEN

Fresh moss covers
the stone bed;
how many springtimes
was it the Master's?

His profile in meditation
has been sketched;
but the body of the meditator
has been burned.

Snow in the pines
has closed the pagoda courtyard;
dust settles in the lock
on the sutra library.

I chide myself
for these two tears—
a man who hasn't grasped
the empty nature of all things.

TO MONK SHAO-MING

Not yet residing
at the Green Dragon Room,
you're midway through fall
in a year of retreat.

From the highest cell
in Sung-shan's old temple,
you can see mist
enveloping rain, below.

How could Hui-k'o have departed
without a word from Bodhidharma?
To show my mind, should I,
like him, cut off my arm?

After Hui-neng,
how many times
will the robe and bowl
be passed on?

贈紹明上人

未住青龍室中秋獨往年上方崧古寺下視雨如煙
祖豈無言去心因斷臂傳不知能已後更有幾燈然

山中道士

頭髮梳千下休糧帶瘦容養雛成大鶴種子作高松白石通宵煮寒泉盡日春不曾離隱處那得世人逢

You've brushed your hair
a thousand strokes;
but your gaunt face shows
you've stopped eating grain.

You raise crane chicks
to full maturity;
plant seeds
to grow tall pines.

A Taoist concoction simmers
through the night;
a cold stream pounds
through the day.

Never far from this
secluded place,
what people of the world
could ever find you?

題竹谷上人院

禪庭高鳥道迴望極川原樵徑連峰頂石泉通竹根

木深猶積雪山淺未聞猿欲別塵中苦願師貽一言

AT THE RETREAT OF MONK CHU-KU

The path to the meditation hall
is steep and perilous;
I look back to view
the upper watershed.

A woodcutter's trail links
all the peaks;
a boulder-choked creek
flows through bamboo.

In deep woods,
the snow still lingers;
in foothills,
gibbons have not yet cried.

Desiring to part from
the bitterness in the world,
I seek one word
from the Master.

MOURNING THE DEATH
OF CH'AN MASTER TSUNG-MI

The trail is dangerous
among snowy, silent peaks.
With the Master gone,
who goes this way to meditation?

Dust slowly gathers
on the tea table;
before his death,
tree colors already had changed.

The pagoda stands
in blowing pines;
footprints fade
along the roaring stream.

Passing by the grieving temple,
the tiger
hears the sutra,
weeps.

哭宗密禪師

鳥道雪岑巔師亡誰去禪几塵增滅後樹色改生前

層塔當松吹殘蹤傍野泉唯嗟聽經虎時到壞菴邊

題李凝幽居

閑居少鄰並草徑入荒園鳥宿池邊樹僧敲月下門

過橋分野色移石動雲根暫去還來此幽期不負言

WRITTEN AT LI NING'S HERMITAGE

A quiet residence
with hardly a neighbor—
a grass-covered path
and deserted garden.

Birds roost
in pond-side trees;
in moonlight,
a monk knocks at a gate.

Crossing a bridge
unfolds more wilderness;
moving a rock
moves the base of clouds.

I've been absent for some time,
but now I'm back;
I won't break our vow
of retreat.

VISITING WITH BUDDHIST MONK WU-K'O
AT HIS REMOTE DWELLING

Ever since your
residence here,
our visits together
have been few.

With the long rains,
the vegetable garden goes untended;
distant mountains shine
in autumn pools.

Withered leaves fall
on your inkstone;
broken clouds
float above your pillow.

A rude guest,
and a future Ch'an Master;
it's not fair
that I cling to our meetings.

辟居無可上人相訪
自從居此地少有事相關積雨荒鄰圃秋池照遠山
硯中枯葉落枕上斷雲閑野客將禪子依依偏往還

題青龍寺鏡公房
一夕曾留宿終南搖落時孤燈岡舍掩殘磬雪風吹
樹老因寒折泉深出井遲疏慵豈有事多失上方期

AT CH'ING-LUNG TEMPLE,
THE MIRROR GUEST ROOM

One evening,
I stayed here overnight,
in the dead-leaf season
of the Chung-nan Mountains.

A lamp from a hidden dwelling
shone from a mountain ridge;
strains of a stone chime
lingered in snow wind.

So bitterly cold,
old trees cracked;
and deep spring water
barely trickled from the well.

Now idle, why
so many worries?
I neglected many things
in my mountain temple days.

YUAN-SHANG AUTUMN RESIDENCE

West of Han-ku Pass,
trees have shed their leaves again;
what am I to do
with these cares of the heart?

I've been down from mountains
a long time;
autumn rains
fall heaviest at night.

Birds fly out
from the mouths of wells;
people from Lo-yang
pass by.

Leaning on my staff,
I gaze a while;
farmers have yet
to cut their grain.

原上秋居
關西又落木心事復如何歲月辭山久秋霖入夜多
鳥從井口出人自岳陽過倚杖柳閑望田家未剪禾

夏木鳥巢邊
過雍秀才居

鐘遠清霄半蜩稀暑雨前幽齋如茸罷約我一來眠
終南嶺色鮮就涼安坐石煮茗汲鄰泉

PASSING BY THE HOME OF SCHOLAR YUNG

In summer trees,
birds stay near their nests;
on the Ch'ung-nan Mountains,
new colors tint the ridges.

In the cool and quiet,
I sit on a rock;
boil lichens with water
drawn from a neighbor's spring.

A distant bell tolls
in the clear air;
a few cicadas sing
before mid-summer rains.

This secluded place,
good as any hut
or thatched pavilion,
invites a nap.

AT SHANG-KU, SEEING OFF A GUEST
TRAVELING RIVERS AND LAKES

Do not grieve
that great distance will separate us;

if the distance were less,
it would still be separation.

In the night, reaching
the river tower, you'll climb,

and over Nan-t'ai
see the moon as before.

上谷送客遊江湖

莫嘆迢遞分何殊咫尺別江樓到夜登還見南台月

墨研秋日雨茶試老僧鐺地近勞頻訪烏紗出送迎
曲江春草生紫閣雪分明汲井嘗泉味聽鐘問寺名
原東居喜唐溫琪頻至

EAST HEIGHTS RESIDENCE,
HAPPY FOR THE FREQUENT VISITS
OF T'ANG WEN-CH'I

Spring grass grows
along Serpentine Lake;
on Purple Pavilion,
the snow is sharp.

We draw our water from the well,
then taste how good the spring;
hear a struck bell,
and ask the temple's name.

On rainy autumn days,
we grind new ink;
make tea
in an old monk's cook pot.

Our houses near,
you take the trouble to visit often;
it's an official's-cap occasion
coming out to greet you, or to see you off.

GETTING UP SICK

Not yet well enough
to return to Sung Mountain;
it's pointless to upbraid myself
for the delay.

How can life's affairs
always go smoothly?
Wild orchids
are already blooming.

Being ill inspires
few new poems;
rain stops old friends
from calling.

Beneath this lamp,
the works of Chuang-tzu,
and a cup of wine
to dispel sorrow.

病起
嵩邱歸未得空自責遲迴身事豈能遂蘭花又已開
病令新作少雨阻故人來燈下南華卷祛愁當酒盃

寄山友長孫栖嶠

此時氣蕭颯琴院可應關鶴似君無事風吹雨遍山

松生青石上泉落白雲間有徑連崧頂心期相與還

SENT TO CHANG-SUN CH'I-CH'IAO,
A MOUNTAIN FRIEND

This time of year,
the weather is chilly;
no need for Lute Courtyard
to be open.

The crane, like you,
has no tangled affairs;
wind blows rain
all through the mountains.

Pines grow on rocks
the color of nature;
streams fall
from between white clouds.

There is a trail
connecting with the summit of Mount Sung;
I still have hopes
of returning there with you.

SENT TO MONK WU-K'O

At your remote temple
there are many tall trees;
with the skies clear,
I think again of visiting.

Stone chimes carry
over ditched field water;
autumn moonlight
enters Ts'ao-t'ang Temple.

Dotted with ants and lichen,
your cave is peaceful;
cicadas outside hide
in dense cypress needles.

You've often thought of traveling
to the sacred mountains;
when will you come
to Sung-shan?

寄無可上人

僻寺多高樹涼天憶重遊磬過溝水盡月入草堂秋
穴蟻苔痕靜藏蟬柏葉稠名山思徧往早晚到嵩丘

哭孟郊

身死聲名在多應萬古傳寡妻無子息破宅帶林泉

塚近登山道詩隨過海船故人相吊後斜日下寒天

LAMENTING THE DEATH OF MENG CHIAO

You are gone
but not the sound of your name;
it deserves
to ring down through the ages.

Your widowed wife
has no children;
your run-down home
has a forest spring.

A mountain path
climbs near your grave;
your poems
go out to all the world.

After old friends
console one another,
the slant sun falls
from the cold sky.

LAMENTING THE DEATH OF MENG TUNG-YEH

The orchid has no fragrance,
and the crane no cry;

autumn days spent mourning—
and the moon no brightness.

Ever since the death
of Tung-yeh,

I've walked and walked
these cloudy hills.

哭孟東野

蘭無香氣鶴無聲哭盡秋天月不明
自從東野先生死側近雲山得散行

秋暮

北門楊柳葉不覺已繽紛值鶴因臨水迎僧忽背雲

白鬢相並出暗淚兩行分默默空朝夕哭吟誰喜聞

AUTUMN DUSK

I didn't realize
that at North Gate,
willow leaves
already whirl and fall.

Because approaching water,
I happen on a crane;
meet a monk, unexpectedly
this side of the clouds.

Your white beard stands out
when we're side by side;
hidden tears make
two separate streaks.

Not a thing to say
after all those days and nights of emptiness.
Who enjoys hearing
these sad songs?

RESPONDING TO SECRETARY YAO HO

Having to travel
far roads because of poverty,
one is able
to keep in touch with old friends.

Excellent wine is easy
to drink up;
good poetry is hard
to respond to in kind.

We used to arrive together
at the Hall of Government Affairs;
then spend the evening
at a friend's.

I wasn't aware of it,
entering the passes late,
but since we parted—
autumn has changed all the trees.

酬姚合校書

因貧行道遠得見舊交遊
美酒易傾盡好詩難卒酬
公堂朝共道私第夜相留
不覺入關晚別來林木秋

言心俱好靜廗暑落暉空歸吏封宵鑰行蛇入古桐

長江頻雨後明月眾星中若任遷人去西浮與剡通

題長江

WRITTEN AT CH'ANG-CHIANG

Sincere words
go with the love of peace;
while I work at the government office,
the sun slips down the sky.

A civil officer, I lock up
and head home in the evening;
a snake enters
the old paulownia tree.

In Ch'ang-chiang,
after long rains—
the moon is bright
in a host of stars.

If banished
from your post, go—
passing through
Buddhist India.

ROWING ON LAKE K'UNG-MING

With one green
bamboo oar,

I glide
through emerald duckweed

(not a fisherman
in sight)

gradually entering
the clear, bright water of autumn.

昆明池泛舟
一枝青竹榜泛泛綠萍裏不見釣魚人漸入秋塘水

One with
the Snowy Night

BOOK   THREE

尋石甕寺上方

野寺入時春雪後崎嶇得到此房前老僧不出迎朝

客已住上方三十年

SEEKING SHIH-WENG TEMPLE'S
HIGHEST HERMITAGE

After spring snow,
I entered the wilderness temple;
climbed a steep mountain path
to stand before this door.

The old monk doesn't come out
to welcome a morning guest;
he's lived in this upper cell
thirty years.

AT THE HUA-SHAN HERMITAGE
OF ADEPT MA TAI

Jade Woman,
"washing her hair in a basin,"
is solitary, high,
indescribable.

Waterfalls spill
from Lotus Peak's summit;
the Yellow River
sweeps past the base of Mount Hua.

Here, small birds break off;
the woods conceal tigers;
gibbons live
where no people do.

After rain:
the autumn moon;
on rock:
old pines and a gate.

馬戴居華山因寄
玉女洗頭盆孤高不可言
絕雀林藏虎無人境有猿秋蟾鏡過雨石上古松門
瀑流蓮岳頂河注華山根

送耿處士

一瓶離別酒未盡即言行萬水千山路孤舟幾月程

川原秋色靜蘆葦晚風鳴迢遞不歸客人傳虛隱名

FAREWELL TO SCHOLAR KENG

A bottle of wine
for parting;
but you're gone
before we can drink it up.

A road of ten thousand rivers
and a thousand peaks—
a lone boat voyaging
how many months?

On a broad river plain,
the colors of autumn bring calm;
in reeds,
the evening wind sings.

Faraway, a traveler
who will never return;
a hidden name gone
from the names passed down by men.

IN EARLY AUTUMN,
SENT TO LING-YIN TEMPLE
ON T'IEN-CHU MOUNTAIN, FOR POSTING

Before the peak, behind the peak,
crisp autumn days at the temple;
from the highest window,
a view of Mount Wo-chou.

Monks in meditation
hear the crickets;
gibbons hang from eaves
where cranes in summer nested.

At night, a mountain bell
carries over the empty river;
the sandbar moon rises
cold at the old stone tower.

The heart has raised its sail,
but the body's yet to follow
to that place where Master Hsieh
walked years ago.

生古石樓心憶懸帆身未遂謝公此地昔年遊
蟋蟀鶴從棲處挂獼猴山鐘夜度空江水汀月寒
峰前峰後寺新秋絶頂高窗見沃州人在定中聞
早秋寄題天竺靈隱寺

松徑僧尋廟沙泉鶴見魚　一川風景好恨不有吾廬

毛女峰當戶日高頭未梳　地侵山影掃葉帶露書

送唐環歸敷水莊

松徑僧尋廟沙泉鶴見魚
一川風景好恨不有吾廬
毛女峰當戶日高頭未梳
地侵山影掃葉帶露書
送唐環歸敷水莊

SENDING OFF T'ANG HUAN,
RETURNING TO A VILLAGE ON THE FU RIVER

Mao-nu Peak
will be your door-leaf view;
though the sun be high,
you won't have brushed your hair.

Gradually mountain shadows
steal over the earth;
leaf-borne dew
spots your writing.

On a path through pines,
a monk searches for a shrine;
a crane watches fish
in a sandy spring.

One river,
a beautiful setting—
a pity I don't have
a thatched hut there.

FOR MONK HUNG-CH'UAN

Under Indigo Mountain,
an old Master,
of undiminished spirit,
washes his feet.

He knows by heart
the plants along the creek;
his dwelling's
in an undisturbed jade wood.

West: the temple lamps
and chimes of evening;
east: the windy woods
and rain of dawn.

That old peak, Mount T'ai-po,
is his neighbor,
rain-wet moss
his stone seat.

贈弘泉上人

洗足下藍嶺古師精進同心知溪卉長居此玉林空

西殿宵燈磬東林曙雨風舊峰鄰太白石座雨苔濛

冬月長安雨中見終南雪

秋節新已盡雨疏露山雪西峰稍覺明殘滴猶
未絶氣侵瀑布水凍著白雲穴今朝灞滻鴈何
夕瀟湘月想彼石房人對雪扉不閉

WINTER MOON, RAIN IN CH'ANG-AN,
WATCHING THE CHUNG-NAN MOUNTAINS
IN SNOW

The Autumn Festival's
already passed;
in light rain,
snowy peaks emerge.

West Summit
briefly brightens;
the rain, a mere drizzle,
still falls.

The invading cold air
freezes waterfalls,
ices the inside
of white-cloud caves.

This morning,
wild geese on the Pa and Ch'an Rivers—
when will they reach
Hsiao and Hsiang river moonlight?

I think of those hermits
in stone houses,
doors open,
facing the snow.

送友人入蜀

萬岑深積翠路向此中難欲暮多羈思因高莫遠看

卓家人寂寞揚子業凋殘惟有岷江水悠悠帶月寒

PARTING FROM A FRIEND ENTERING SHU

Ten thousand high pointed hills
run deep and storied and blue;
and the road is treacherous
through all of it—through Shu.

When dusk falls,
you push back anxious thoughts;
because of the surrounding heights,
you can't see far.

Descendants of Cho Wen-chun
are long silent;
and Yang Hsiung's calling
continues, in decline.

All you have before you
is the Min:
vast and unhurried
in cold moonlight.

FAREWELL TO MONK HO-LAN

When you, O wild monk,
come to say good-bye,
we sit for a while
by the sandy creek.

On far roads,
you hold out an empty bowl;
deep in mountains,
walk on fallen flowers.

Having no master, you
puzzle out Ch'an on your own;
observing strict prosody,
your poems merit praise.

This going away
has no circumstantial cause;
a solitary cloud
just has no fixed home.

送賀蘭上人
野僧來別我略坐傍泉沙
遠道擎空缽深山踏落花
無師禪自解有格句堪誇
此去非緣事孤雲不定家

宿贊上人房

階前多是竹閒地擬栽松朱點草書疏雪平麻履蹤

御溝寒夜雨宮寺靜時鐘此室無他事來尋不厭重

OVERNIGHT AT MONK YUN'S ROOM

A thicket of bamboo
before the steps—
a fallow field
where you want to plant pine.

Dots of red ink
mark the grass writing;
tracks of hemp sandals
leave prints on the snow.

Cold night rain
on the imperial canal—
a quiet bell
at the palace temple.

This room
has nothing extraneous;
those who come here searching
never tire of revering you.

SENT TO MO-KUNG ON PAI-KO PEAK

I've already heard
you're back on White Pavilion;
through the rain-rinsed air,
I can see that far peak.

In a stone dwelling,
a man with a quiet heart;
on frozen ponds,
shadows of the waning moon.

Small clouds, one by one,
break up, dissolve;
old trees fall
for firewood.

In the depths of night,
who hears the stone chimes?
It's cold
on West Peak's highest crag.

寄白閣默公
已知歸白閣山遠晚晴看石室人心靜冰潭月影殘
微雲分片滅古木落薪乾後夜誰聞磬西峰絶頂寒

送褚山人歸日東

懸帆待秋水去入杳冥
岸遙生白髮波盡露青山

關東海幾年別中華此日還
隔水相思在無書也是閑

SEEING OFF THE MOUNTAIN MONK CH'U,
RETURNING TO JAPAN

Sail spread, you're ready
to depart on autumn waters,
to enter a deep, far realm
between realms.

Absent from the Eastern Sea
so many years—
today your return
begins on the Yellow River.

While far from home,
your hair's turned white;
but at wave's end,
blue hills will arise.

Separated by water,
we'll be in each other's thoughts—
but no letters to disturb
a monk's quiet life.

THINKING OF A FRIEND
TRAVELING TO THE BORDER

Frozen in sadness
before a single candle—
just yesterday, we drank a cup
to farewell.

With leaves underfoot,
an old friend departs;
in the heavens,
the first geese arrive.

Endless river sands,
sparse fall grass—
dusk bringing snow
to the mountains.

North of the Yuan River,
your way is through red dust;
When will you return
from afar?

思遊邊友人
凝愁對孤燭昨日飲離杯
葉下故人去天中新鴈來
連沙秋草薄帶雪暮山開
苑北紅塵道何時見遠迴

晴湖勝鏡碧寒柳似金黃若有相思夢殷勤載八行
高城滿夕陽何事欲霓裳遷客蓬蒿暮遊人道路長
送人適越

SEEING OFF A FRIEND TRAVELING TO YUEH

The high-walled city
fills with light of the setting sun.
What has brought you
to this downcast state?

A banished official
in the wilderness dusk—
a traveler
on a long, long road.

When the rains stop,
lakes will mirror the blue sky,
winter willows
will shoot forth, golden.

In dreams,
if we meet,
let's be diligent and write
our eight-line, new-style poems.

AT CH'UNG-SHENG TEMPLE,
PIN-KUNG'S ROOM

Lately, you're eating
only once a day;
in the trees,
the door of your Ch'an retreat is shut.

With the sun going down,
a cold stone chime sounds on the mountain;
you wear a monk's robe
ragged with the years.

On your temples,
there's more white to shave;
light blue clouds
return from far away.

You still speak
of a trip to sacred Nan-yueh,
how walking meditation
quiets little mind.

崇聖寺彬公房

近來惟一食樹下掩禪扉落日寒山磬多年壞衲衣

白鬚多更剃青靄遠還歸仍說遊南岳經行是息機

雨夜寄馬戴

芳林杏花樹花落子西東今夕曲江雨寒催朔北風

鄉書滄海絕隱路翠微通寂寂相思際孤缸殘漏中

RAINY NIGHT, SENT TO MA TAI

The woods are the fragrance
of blossoming apricot trees;
flowers scatter seed
east and west.

Rain this evening
on Serpentine Lake—
a north wind
blows hard and cold.

Letters go as far
as the blue sea and stop:
a hidden road
winds through mountain haze.

By a lone lamp,
in the hours before dawn,
quietly
I'm thinking of you.

94

FAREWELL TO A T'IEN-T'AI MONK

You've long dreamed
of going back to Hua-shan;
your small boat leaves
Yueh-yang Stream.

You observe pure meals—
wild plants and fruit;
night waves
rock your meditation seat.

At dawn,
wild geese cross a lone peak;
gibbons cry
from frozen woods.

I have no special names
of Buddha to intone;
my remaining practice
is this verse.

送天台僧

遠夢歸華頂扁舟背岳陽寒蔬修淨食夜浪動禪床
鴈過孤峰曉猿啼一樹霜身心無別念餘習在詩章

雨夜同屬玄懷皇甫荀

桐竹遠庭匝雨多風更吹還如舊山夜臥聽瀑泉時

磧鴈來期近秋鐘到夢遲溝西吟苦客中夕話兼思

RAINY NIGHT WITH LI HSUAN,
RECALLING HUANG FU-HSUN

Paulownia trees, bamboo
surround the courtyard;
the rain is heavy
and the wind increasing.

This night is like those
in past mountains
when, lying in bed,
I'd listen to cascading streams,

about the time of year
when wild geese migrate,
and the fall temple bell
comes slowly to one's dreams.

West of the waterway,
a traveler is writing a poem;
throughout the evening,
our talk of him unites us.

EVENING GATHERING
AT THE RESIDENCE OF YAO HO;
K'O-KUNG DOES NOT ARRIVE

At the Hall of Government Affairs,
a rainy night in spring,
and we're already thinking of
gardens and trees.

We inquire after the health
of old friends,
then speak of the nature
of mountains and streams.

A lone lamp shines
after winter sacrifice;
a light snow
deepens on the ground.

Monk K'o-kung
has turned back from our appointment;
only cold stone chimes
come from West Spring.

夜集姚合宅期可公不至
公堂秋雨夜已是念園林何事疾病日重論山水心
孤燈明臘後微雪下更深釋子乖來約泉西寒磬音

97

寄長武朱尚書

不日即登壇槍旗一萬竿角吹邊月沒鼓絕爆雷殘

中國今如此西荒可取難白衣思請謁徒步在長安

SENT TO SECRETARY CH'ANG WU-CHU

Without a word,
they ascend the sacrificial altar,
facing flags, lances and
ten thousand bamboo spears.

A bugle blows
as the border moon sets;
drums break off
their lethal thunder.

This is the Middle Kingdom
today;
the desolate West
has proved hard to subdue.

You, wise sir,
should consider asking for an audience
and go on foot
to the capital, Ch'ang-an.

FAREWELL TO A MILITARY ENLISTEE,
ON THE ROAD

You say farewell, about to go
into the wild grasses of the plain;
sun at a slant, a shrike
in the air.

At Dragon Gate,
the River I races;
one high cloud floats
over Sung-shan's peaks.

You've often complained
of having no close friends,
that your hair's already
turning gray.

Now, you've enlisted in the army,
so take this road and go—
be like the wind-driven waves
rising on the sea at Kuang-ling.

送路某從軍

別我就蓬蒿日斜飛伯勞龍門流水急嵩嶽片雲高

嘆命無知己梳頭落白毛從軍當此去風起廣陵濤

99

送慈恩寺霄韻法師謁太原李司空

清磬先寒角禪燈徹曉烽舊房閑片石倚著最高松
何故謁司空雲山知幾重磧遙來鴈盡雪急去僧逢

SEEING OFF BUDDHIST MASTER HSIA-YUN
OF T'SE-EN TEMPLE TO AN AUDIENCE
WITH MINISTER OF PUBLIC WORKS LI,
AT T'AI-YUAN, CAPITAL OF SHANSI

What reason to have an audience
with Public Works?
You know it means ranges
of cloudy mountains to cross.

Wild geese have quit coming
from far sand shallows;
entering T'ai-yuan,
you meet fast-flying snow.

Pure stone chimes and
cold bugles answer each other;
signal fires, meditation lamps
burn through dawn.

Your old hermitage
of irregular-placed stone
stands crooked against
the tallest pine.

OVERNIGHT AT CH'ING-YEH TEMPLE
WITH LI K'UO,
FORMER HU DISTRICT SUB-PREFECT

You've come from the mountains
above town,
and we meet at the temple
in the capital at dusk.

Again and again,
our conversation lapses;
a light rain
drips in the pines.

Your family is poor
and you've just been removed from office;
you've grown old and recoil
at hearing the cricket's call.

As if still constrained
by the customs of office,
you rise and dress hastily
when the dawn bell tolls.

淨業寺與前鄠縣李廓少府同宿
來從城上峰京寺暮相逢往往語復默
家貧初罷吏年長畏聞蛩前日猶拘束披衣起曉鐘
微微雨灑松

贈李金州

綺里祠前後山程踐白雲沂流隨大旆登岸見全軍

曉角吹人夢秋風卷鴈群霧開方露日漢水底沙分

FOR LI OF CHIN-CHOU

Before the shrine to Ch'i Li
and after the shrine,
the mountain road
treads on white clouds.

Against the stream,
large flags and pennants come;
from the riverbank,
the whole army can be seen.

At dawn, a bugle
blows in the soldiers' dreams;
the autumn wind buffets
a flock of geese.

Mist parts,
and the sun streams through;
on the Han riverbed,
pebbles and sand are clear.

TRAVEL STOP ON THE HAN RIVER

At Hsi-chia's ponds and lowlands,
the grass grows lush and wild;

in misted light, I ride
my horse easy through the trees.

The shrine to Liu Pei faces
blue waters of the River Hsiang;

at sunset: a bugle-like cry
in the wind.

行次漢上
習家池沼草萋萋嵐樹光中信馬蹄
漢主廟前湘水碧一聲風角夕陽低

冬夜

羈旅復經冬瓢空盎亦空淚流寒枕上跡絕舊山中
凌結浮萍水雪和衰柳風曙光雞未報嘹唳兩三鴻

WINTER NIGHT

Again winter catches out
a traveler far from home—
the cook pot's empty
and the ladle, too.

Tears streak
a cold pillow;
human tracks
end in old mountains.

Ice forms
on the duckweed stream;
snow flies
in a bare willow wind.

Chickens still haven't announced
the first light of day
when I hear the cries
of two or three wild swans.

SEEING OFF CH'AN MASTER HUI-YA
RETURNING TO JADE SPRINGS

You've only gone as far
as the Hsiao and Hsiang Rivers,
and have yet to travel
Tung-t'ing Lake.

Drinking water from a spring,
you watch the setting moon;
below the gorges,
hear the gibbons cry.

Rain and thunder
do not stop your teaching;
nearing the sea flow,
you chant sacred verses.

The evening dew has fallen
when you return to Ch'u;
the autumn stars are frosty
over Jade Springs.

送惠雅法師歸玉泉
祇到瀟湘水洞庭湖未遊
飲泉看月別下峽聽猿愁
講不停雷雨吟當近海流
降霜歸楚夕星冷玉泉秋

靜語終燈燄餘生許嶠雲猶來多抱疾聲不達明君
僧同雪夜坐鴈向草堂聞
十里尋幽寺寒流數派分
就可松宿

OVERNIGHT STAY WITH K'O-KUNG

For ten *li*
I've been searching for the hidden temple
up branches
of the cold stream.

Monks sit Ch'an,
one with the snowy night;
wild geese, approaching Ts'ao-t'ang,
fly within hearing.

With lamp flames dying,
our words are subdued;
the rest of our lives
should be clouds and high peaks.

Up to now,
I've been sick a lot,
and the Enlightened Prince
does not know my name.

FAREWELL TO MONK WU-K'O

After the weather clears,
the slopes of Kuei-feng have new color;
I've come to see you off—the monk
of Ts'ao-t'ang Temple.

We talk as we leave the grounds,
a fly-whisk in your hand;
amid the sound of crickets,
we're unwilling to part.

A lone shadow
walks on the bottom of a pond;
someone,
now and then, rests beside a tree.

In the end, we'll meet
in the colored clouds and haze;
I'll be your closest neighbor
on T'ien-t'ai.

送無可上人

圭峰霽色新　送此草堂人
塵尾同離寺　蛩鳴暫別親
獨行潭底影　數息樹邊身
終有煙霞約　天台作近鄰

口
號

申夜忽自起汲此百尺泉林木含白露星斗在青天

POEM JUST JOTTED DOWN

In the middle of the night,
I suddenly rise;

draw water
from the deep well.

White dew
covers the woods;

morning stars
dot the clear sky.

Short Glossary of
Recurring Words and Symbols

Ch'an, or *Zen.* Both are used interchangeably to refer to the transmission of understanding begun in China by Bodhidharma. Chinese Buddhists adopted the word Ch'an from the Sanskrit *dhyana,* meaning broadly "meditation." See also *zazen.*

Ch'ing. A stone chime, or gong, consisting of a piece of flat, sonorous stone or metal. The *ch'ing* is used as a gong in Buddhist temples, or as a percussion instrument elsewhere. It was especially used to bring meditators gently out of deep meditation. The sound of a bell was customarily thought to be too abrupt and harsh.

Crane. A symbol of longevity or immortality. A "wild crane" is a recluse.

Lamp. A solace to the traveler and a stand-in for the moon.

Li. A Chinese mile, roughly equivalent to one-third of an English mile.

Moon. A comforting light and symbol of enlightenment.

Sacred mountains of China. There are five: Hua Mountain, located in Shensi Province; Mount T'ai in Shansi; Mount Sung in Honan; Mount Heng in Shensi; and Mount Heng (written with a different Chinese character) in Hunan. The four sacred Buddhist mountains are Mount Wu-t'ai in Shansi; Mount Chiu-hua in

Anhui; Mount P'u-t'o, an island off the coast of Chekiang; and Mount Omei in Szechuan.

Sea. Translation for the Chinese word *hai,* which can be any broad expanse of water.

Shan. Technically it is redundant to say, for instance, "Mount Sung-shan," since *shan* means "mountain" (or "hill"). In these translations, I have written the names in a variety of ways: Mount Sung, Sung Mountain, Sung-shan.

Sutra. Sermons of the Buddha or of his enlightened disciples.

White Clouds. The world of eremites on one level, and the inner world on another.

Wild Geese. Often a symbol of letters or communication.

Willows. A symbol of parting.

Zazen, **sit Ch'an, quiet sitting, sitting**, or **meditation.** I use these terms interchangeably for the practice of Zen meditation.

Notes to Colors of Daybreak and Dusk (Book One)

Sent to Minister Ling-hu, p. 14

Minister Ling-hu, or Ling Hu-ch'u, was a highly respected scholar-official and friend of Chia Tao. This poem was possibly written about Chia Tao's journey of exile from Ch'ang-an, the capital, to *Ch'ang-chiang,* a T'ang county in today's Szechuan Province. There, at the age of fifty-nine, Chia Tao assumed the minor post of Registrar. The town of *Tzu-chou* was near Ch'ang-chiang. See the poem "Written at Ch'ang-chiang," p. 74.

Winter Night Farewell, p. 15

Ch'u was a large and powerful state that existed 740–223 B.C. It occupied the middle Yangtze River area in the south and stretched as far north as the upper reaches of the Huai River. The *Ch'u Mountains* are in present-day Hunan Province.

Memento on the Departure of a Friend From Yeh,
Last Day of the Second Moon, p. 16

Yeh was the ancient name for a part of what is today Honan Province. *Willows* are a symbol of parting. *Mist,* or *fog,* in the lowlands generally moves like a tide up river valleys in the afternoon. Chia Tao is reminding his friend of this to discourage delay.

Morning Travel, p. 17

The *bell* is the just-before-dawn summons of a Buddhist temple. Red Pine interprets this poem as depicting Chia Tao's departure from monastic life: the *journey* is into the secular world; the *chickens* are the other monks; the *innkeeper* is the Ch'an Master; and the *slipping*, the unsure footing of the poet.

Passing by a Mountain Village at Dusk, p. 18

A *li* is about one-third of a mile. *Border signal towers* employed lighted beacons to communicate between detachments guarding China's borders. Apparently, the poet is traveling outside *Ch'in*, the T'ang Dynasty name for China. In their cultivation, silkworms feed on leaves of the *mulberry* tree; the *chih* is a thorny, hardwood tree of some fifteen feet in height whose bark contains a yellow pigment. Its leaves are an alternative food for silkworms. *Cook smoke (yen-huo)* here suggests human warmth.

Overnight at a Mountain Monastery, p. 19

Cranes and *pines* are associated with longevity and immortality. In Bill Porter's *Road to Heaven: Encounters with Chinese Hermits* (chapter 1, p. 12) another Buddhist monk is spoken of: "One of the mountains we visited was Tailaoshan....A Buddhist layman we met on the trail led us to a cave where an eighty-five-year-old monk had been living for the past fifty years. In the course of our conversation, the monk asked me who this Chairman Mao was whom I kept mentioning."

Farewell to Monk Chih-hsing, p. 20

Although *Pa-hsing*, the temple, is not identified, a county of that name existed during the T'ang Dynasty in Szechuan Province. *Buddhist staff (hsi-chang)*: a monk's walking stick, often fitted with metal rings for shaking to announce one's presence and to drive away demons. *Sea (hai)* can be any substantial expanse of water, though here—owing to the characterization of the rising sun as *miniature*—the expanse might very well be the East China Sea. This would probably place *Monk Chih-hsing's* intended site of retreat in the T'ien-t'ai Mountains.

At I-chou, Climbing the Tower of Lung-hsing Temple
to View the High Northern Mountains, p. 22

In the T'ang-dynasty, the prefecture of I *(I-chou)* was located along the Szechuan-Hopei Road. Today, the county of I *(I-hsien)* lies within Hopei Province. *Lung-hsing Temple* is not identified.

Seeking but Not Finding the Recluse, p. 23

This is Chia Tao's most famous poem, known to the West through its inclusion in the Ch'ing Dynasty collection, the *Three Hundred Poems of the T'ang.* The poem has been described as a twenty-syllable evocation of the heart and soul of China's eremitic tradition.

Abode of the Unplanned Effect, p. 25

The *abode* was near, or on the grounds of, Sheng-tao Temple on a high plateau in a ward of the same name in southeast Ch'ang-an. The *Chung-nan Mountains,* south-southwest of Ch'ang-an, are the divide of north and south China (see introduction). The person in the poem wears a *common white robe,* hence he is not a monk. *Calming of the heart* is my rendering of *wang-chi,* or "forgetting schemes or designs in one's mind," a Buddhist meditation practice.

A Farewell to T'ien Cho on Retreat on Hua Mountain, p. 26

Hua Mountain, located in Shensi Province, is one of the five sacred peaks of China, the others being Mount T'ai in Shansi, Mount Sung in Honan, Mount Heng in Shensi, and Mount Heng (a different Chinese character) in Hunan. The four sacred Buddhist mountains are Mount Wu-t'ai in Shansi, Mount Chiu-hua in Anhui, Mount P'u-t'o, an island off the coast of Chekiang, and Mount Omei in Szechuan. An *immortal (hsien)* was often depicted as riding on a flying crane. Chia Tao is encouraging, and expects, his friend to "make immortal."

Seeing Off Sub-Prefect Mu to Mei-chou, p. 29

Mei-chou is located in Mei-shan County in today's Szechuan Province. *Sword Gate*, or *Chien-men*, is a pass in the Ta-chien Mountains through which one leaves the inner provinces to enter Szechuan. The *Han River* is a tributary of the Yangtze. The *gorges* are likely the famed gorges of the Yangtze River, inhabited by the gibbon, a small tailless ape with a haunting shriek or cry. The *climbing vines* are *hsueh-lo: Ficus pumila*, a rubber plant.

Overnight in Ch'eng-hsiang Forest, p. 31

Water clock (*lou* or *lou-k'e*) is a Chinese instrument that measured time by the flow of water. Also known as a clepsydra.

Farewell to Master Tan Returning to Min, p. 32

Min, a Ten Kingdoms state (tenth century), was roughly in the same area as present-day Fukien Province. During the T'ang Dynasty, *Lo-yang* was the summer eastern capital for nearly three hundred years. *To wash or bathe before sitting* can be understood as a symbolic purification. *Yueh*, an ancient state of the Eastern Chou period (770–256 B.C.), included part of today's Chekiang Province.

At Ni-yang Inn, p. 33

Ni-yang was a county seat north of Ch'ang-an. *White dew (pai-lu)* is also one of the twenty-four Chinese solar terms, and falls in our Gregorian calendar around September 8.

Farewell to a Friend Leaving for the Frontier, p. 34

Double Nine (Cheng-yang) is a festival celebrated on the ninth day of the ninth lunar month. It is principally a day dedicated to the elderly. Friends use the occasion to climb hills or mountains, compose poetry, and drink tea or wine. It is also associated with chrysanthemums, the "flower of autumn." The headwaters of the *Han River* lie in southern Shensi Province. The river flows through Hupei Province and meets the Yangtze River near Hankow. It is the Yangtze's largest and longest tributary.

Thinking of Retired Scholar Wu on the River, p. 36

Chia Tao indicates the moon by *ch'an-ch'u,* or "the toad that lives in the moon." The couplet "Autumn wind arises on Wei River / falling leaves fill Ch'ang-an" is famous in part for this anecdote: Chia Tao was riding a donkey through the streets of Ch'ang-an (as in the tale describing how he met Han Yu), deeply absorbed in finding a parallel line to "falling leaves fill Ch'ang-an." He got the line, but accidentally collided with a city official who had him briefly jailed. This anecdote—as well as the one alluded to above—was used as evidence by at least one critic of a later dynasty to attack Chia Tao as a heretic of the poetics of direct experience and realism, and to accuse him of moving in the direction of poetic stylization—a theoretically pure position, but impractical even for its proponents—certainly not a substantial, chargeable offense. *Wei River* flows east past Ch'ang-an in Shen-si Province and is the major tributary of the Yellow River. *Orchid-wood oar (lan-nao)* signifies a boat.

Happy that Official Yao Is Returning from Hang-chou, p. 37

Official Yao, the poet Yao Ho, was returning to the capital to assume a new government post. *Hang-chou* was the southern terminus of the canal that carried silk and grain to the summer capital of Lo-yang. *Cloud Gate* is a mountain near Shao-hsing, southeast of Hang-chou in Chekiang Province. It is historically associated with Buddhism. Presumably, if Chia Tao had met his friend at Cloud Gate, he would have been able to enjoy the boat ride with Yao Ho.

Late in the Day, Gazing Out from a River Pavilion, p. 38

The third stanza seems indebted to the *Confucian Analects,* Chapter XXI: "The wise find pleasure in water; the virtuous, in mountains."

Auspicious Arrival of Yung T'ao, p. 39

Yung T'ao, a native of Chengtu, the capital city of Szechuan, was a poet and successful candidate of the Civil Service Examination who received the title of *po-shih*, conferred upon scholars of profound learning. *Sword Gate:* see note to the poem "Seeing Off Sub-Prefect Mu to Mei-chou" (p. 114). *The Lu River* is an upper branch of the Yangtze River.

Seeing Off the Monk Ts'ung-ch'ih Returning to the Capital, p. 40
Western Light, or *Hsi-ming,* was a temple near Ch'ang-an's South (Red Bird) Gate in the ward of Yen-k'ang.

Response to Sub-Prefect Li K'uo of Hu County, p. 41
Witzling notes that "a sub-prefect in the provinces would be in charge of assembling raw materials to supply the court's needs." *Li K'uo,* an official and a friend of Chia Tao's, makes another appearance in "Overnight at Ch'ing-yeh Temple with Li K'uo." *Hu County* was located in the southwest of what is today's Ch'ang-an County in Shensi Province. *South Mountain:* Chung-nan Mountain. These *bamboo fences (li)* are woven of living bamboo. Here, they suggest the fences of farmers in mountain valleys. *Blue-sea companion* is a traveling companion. *White-cloud master:* a bureaucrat, or high official. *Wild crane:* a recluse.

Overnight at Hsuan-ch'uan Courier Station, p. 42
Li-shui Tower is unidentified. *Hsuan-ch'uan* is located at the head-waters of the Chi River. *The Chi River,* in Honan Province, empties into the Yellow River. The *mountain lamp* is that of a mountain recluse. A lamp, like the moon, can be a symbol of enlightenment or Buddha nature, but in Chia Tao's poems, objects' meanings are usually naturalistic.

Spring Travel, p. 43
Courtesans is my choice of translation for *hsien-hua;* however, the first meaning of *hsien-hua* is "motionless flowers."

Notes to The Tiger Hears the Sutra (Book Two)

Ferrying Across the Dry Mulberry River, p. 46

The Dry Mulberry River (*Sang-kan-shui*) is known today as the Yung-ting-shui. *Ping-chou* is located in today's Shansi Province in the county of T'ai-yuan. In the Chinese text, Chia Tao uses the name *Ch'eng-yang* to refer to Ch'ang-an, now called Xi'an (or Sian). Ch'eng-yang was also the name of a county near Ch'ang-an, north of the Wei River.

Taking Leave of a Buddhist Master, Departing China, p. 47

Yueh was an ancient state that occupied the present-day provinces of Fukien and Chekiang. As Witzling discusses, the second stanza implies that on his journey, the Buddhist master eats only one bowl of rice every third day.

Seeing Off Shen-miao, Buddhist Master, p. 48

Western Szechuan, or *Hsi-chou* in the Chinese text.

Seeing Off a Man of the Tao, p. 49

A *white dog* was symbolically associated with Taoist masters.

Sent to a Hua Mountain Monk, p. 50

Hua Mountain: see glossary. *The clouds that arise* are not metaphorical, but rather the afterimages stimulated by the constant real clouds in the monk's mountain environment. *Bells* is plural because several temples existed in the area. The fifth-watch bell is struck just before dawn.

For a Buddhist Monk, p. 51

The *magic dragon pearl* is a symbol of enlightenment. Depending on the variant characters in the texts of Chia Tao's poems, of which there are many, one could translate any number of lines differently. The first two lines of the second stanza, for instance, could be translated (rather flatly): "A Buddhist staff / hangs from an overlook to the sea." In the Chinese text *Wu-hu* (Five Lakes) refers to *T'ai-hu* (Lake T'ai), located on the borders of Kiangsu and Chekiang Provinces, but it could also be shorthand for "five lakes, four seas," meaning all of China—ergo, the world. In any case, neither the *affairs of Five Lakes,* nor the world's affairs, are the talk of these mountain recluses.

Seeing Off a Buddhist Monk Traveling to Heng Mountain, p. 52
Heng Mountain in Hunan. There are two sacred Heng mountains—one in the north and one in the south (but their names are different Chinese characters). The southern one in this poem was the site of Nan-yueh Monastery, from which came Hui Ssu, the Second Patriarch of the Buddhist T'ien-t'ai sect, as well as Shih-tou, the patriarch of the Soto Zen sect. *Temple chimes (ch'ing):* see glossary.

Sent to Monks Chen and K'ung at Lung-ch'ih Temple, p. 53
Lung-ch'ih (Dragon Pond) *Temple* is located in the Chung-nan Mountains. See note to "Abode of the Unplanned Effect" (p. 113). *Stone Bridge* is presumably a landmark on the temple grounds. Witzling reasons that the monks are unable to leave the temple because they are on retreat.

Mourning the Death of Ch'an Master Po-yen, p. 54
Master Po-yen, or Monk Huai-hui, died in 816 (the tenth year of the Yuan-ho Period of Emperor Hsien-tsung). The *pagoda* is where the body of the Master was cremated, and the *sutra* (Buddhist scripture) *library* is where the sketched profile is preserved. *Sunyata:* emptiness (the immateriality of all things). A portion of D.T. Suzuki's translation of the *Heart Sutra* from his *Manual of Zen Buddhism* reads: "O Sariputra, form is here emptiness, emptiness is form; form is no other than emptiness, emptiness is no other than form; that which is form is emptiness; that which is emptiness is

form." Suzuki points out that "*sunyata* is one of the most important notions in Mahayana philosophy and at the same time the most puzzling for non-Buddhist readers to comprehend."

To Monk Shao-ming, p. 55

Sung-shan, southeast of Lo-yang, is the sacred mountain on which *Bodhidharma* meditated for nine years at Shao-lin Temple. He is the First Patriarch *(tsu)* of Ch'an (or Zen) Buddhism. *Hui-k'o,* as recounted in the *Transmission of the Lamp,* stood outside Bodhidharma's cave many days—even through a snow storm—hoping to meet with him, but the Master refused. Hui-k'o then cut off his arm to further demonstrate his serious purpose. The Master relented. Hui-k'o eventually became the Second Patriarch of Zen. *Hui-neng* was an illiterate kitchen helper who became the Sixth Patriarch of Zen. See the *Platform Sutra of the Sixth Patriarch,* translated by Philip B. Yampolsky.

Taoist Master in Mountains, p. 56

The act of brushing hair here suggests both daily ritual and a concern for grooming despite the retreat to the wilderness. *Taoist concoction:* literally "white rocks," the fare of recluses. In translating, I chose the word "concoction" to hint at alchemy and/or pharmacology, which included minerals as well as herbs.

At the Retreat of Monk Chu-ku, p. 58

The path is *steep and perilous (niao-tao):* literally, a "bird way." While the poem is Ch'an in feeling, "I seek one word / from the Master" echoes the first line of Book xv, Chapter xxii, of the *Confucian Analects.*

Mourning the Death of Ch'an Master Tsung-mi, p. 59

Master Kuei-feng Tsung-mi (780–841) was the Fifth Patriarch of the Hua-yen (Flower Garland) school of Ch'an (known later in Japan as Kegon). This school emphasized the *Avatamsaka Sutra (Flower Garland Sutra),* an important Mahayana scripture said to be the only teaching expounded by the Buddha during his enlightenment. See Thomas Cleary's *Entry into the Inconceivable: An Introduction to Hua-yen Buddhism,* as well as his translation, *The Flower Ornament Sutra. The trail is dangerous (niao-tao):* see the notes to the preceding poem.

Written at Li Ning's Hermitage, p. 60
"In moonlight, / a monk knocks at a gate." See the introduction.

Visiting with Buddhist Monk Wu-k'o at His Remote Dwelling, p. 61
Monk Wu-k'o was Chia Tao's cousin and a highly regarded poet-monk. He also had the name K'o-kung. He is mentioned in three other poems, all in the third section of this volume.

At Ch'ing-lung Temple, the Mirror Guest Room, p. 62
Ch'ing-lung Temple, or Green Dragon Temple, in a southern ward of Ch'ang-an, faces the Chung-nan Mountains to the south.

Yuan-shang Autumn Residence, p. 63
Yuan-shang is a high plateau in southeast Ch'ang-an in Sheng-tao Ward. Sheng-tao Temple is located there. The *Chung-nan Mountains,* south–southwest of Ch'ang-an, are the north–south divide of China. See the poem "Abode of the Unplanned Effect" (p. 25). The land *west of Han-ku Pass,* designated *Kuan-hsi* in the Chinese text, includes Shensi and Kansu Provinces. *People from Lo-yang* might refer to the people (officials and the like) returning to the capital, Ch'ang-an, from the summer capital of Lo-yang.

Passing by the Home of Scholar Yung, p. 64
The *Ch'ung-nan Mountains.* See the note to the preceding poem.

At Shang-ku, Seeing Off a Guest Traveling Rivers and Lakes, p. 65
Shang-ku is in northeast Hopei Province, where Chia Tao was born, near today's Beijing. *Nan-t'ai,* or South Tower, is on the grounds of Sheng-tao Temple in southeast Ch'ang-an.

East Heights Residence, Happy for the Frequent Visits
of T'ang Wen-ch'i, p. 66

    Serpentine Lake (Ch'u-chiang) was an artificial lake built for
Emperor Wu-ti in the first century B.C. in southeast Ch'ang-an.
It was the setting for Tu Fu's (712–770) famous poems "Ballad
of Lovely Women" and "Riverside Lament." In Chia Tao's day it
was apparently a good locale for the reclusive-minded. Today
the lake is farmland, although there are plans underway for
restoring it to a park. *Purple Pavilion Peak* is located southeast of
Ch'ang-an in the Mount Kuei-feng massif. In the last stanza,
Chia Tao employs the idea of wearing an official's cap to wel-
come and see off T'ang Wen-ch'i to underline the importance
he attaches to his friend. The idea also works, of course, to
humorously juxtapose a symbol of state with idle, reclusive life.

Getting Up Sick, p. 67

    The poem may allude to the *Vimalakirti Sutra. Sung Mountain*,
located in Honan, is one of the five sacred mountains. See glos-
sary. *Chuang-tzu* (369–286 B.C.), or Chuang-chou, was a major
Taoist philospher, contemporary with Mencius.

Sent to Chang-sun Ch'i-ch'iao, a Mountain Friend, p. 68

    Mount Sung: see the note to the preceding poem.

Sent to Monk Wu-k'o, p. 69

    Monk Wu-k'o, also called K'o-kung, was Chia Tao's cousin and
a poet-monk of high reputation. *Ts'ao-t'ang* (literally, thatched
hut, or humble cottage used by hermits) is the name of a tem-
ple just below Mount Kuei-feng in today's Shensi Province. At
the time, Chia Tao was staying on Sung Mountain, where the
famous poet Meng Chiao (751–814; see the introduction) also
lived in reclusion for a number of years.

Lamenting the Death of Meng Chiao, p. 70

    Meng Chiao (751–814) was a famous Mid-T'ang Dynasty poet.

See the introduction and the notes to the preceding poem.

Lamenting the Death of Meng Tung-yeh, p. 71
 Meng Tung-yeh is another name for Meng Chiao. See the note
 to the preceding poem.

Autumn Dusk, p. 72
 North Gate is the North Gate of Ch'ang-an. Chia Tao is sur-
 prised to find his friend, the monk, down from the clouds after
 a long period of retreat. The monk's tears and silence bring to
 mind Witzling's discussion of Wang Wei's poem "Passing the
 Ch'ing-lung Monastery on a Summer Day to Visit the Ch'an
 Master Ts'ao." Wang Wei mentions *k'ung-ping,* the ailment of
 emptiness, and Witzling explains that "to suffer from the ail-
 ment of emptiness is to go too far in denying the existence of
 things; it must be remembered that things exist in some senses
 and not in others." While the monk in this poem may be suffer-
 ing such an ailment, it should be noted that the full Wang Wei
 phrase reads *"k'ung-ping k'ung,"* or "the ailment of emptiness is
 empty"—it has no permanent existence. *Songs (k'u-yin)* literal-
 ly means "bitter singing," but as Witzling points out, it is a term
 Chia Tao also uses to indicate the act of composing a poem.

Responding to Secretary Yao Ho, p. 73
 Yao Ho, a poet, official, and close friend of Chia Tao. See the poem
 "Happy that Official Yao Is Returning from Hang-chou" (p. 37).
 The passes are the mountain passes leading back to Ch'ang-an.

Written at Ch'ang-chiang, p. 74
 Ch'ang-chiang was a T'ang county located in today's Sui-ning
 County in Szechuan Province. Chia Tao was transferred there to
 serve in the minor post of Registrar. The poem indicates that
 he had, in fact, suffered some form of banishment. Slander of the
 court was the probable offense, but it has also been suggested that
 Chia Tao was not the perpetrator of slander, but its victim. The

famous Sung Dynasty poet Su Tung P'o was also banished on charges of slander and, like Chia Tao, assigned to an insignificant post in the provinces.

Rowing on Lake K'ung-ming, p. 75
Lake K'ung-ming, in Shensi Province, was a man-made lake dug by order of the Emperor Wu of the Han Dynasty. It was six or seven miles west of Sian, within the precincts of the royal palace.

Notes to One with the Snowy Night (Book Three)

At the Hua-shan Hermitage of Adept Ma Tai, p. 79

Hua-shan: a sacred mountain in Shensi Province historically asso-
ciated with Taoism. *Ma Tai* (mid-ninth century) was a success-
ful candidate of the civil service examination *(chin-shih)* and
served in official posts. He was also a good poet and, periodi-
cally, a hermit. He left behind ninety to one hundred poems. *Jade
Woman,* the name of the central peak of Hua Mountain, derives
from the name of King Mu's daughter Nung Yu, or "[she who]
plays with jade," of the state of Ch'in. Nung Yu lived on the
mountain with her husband Hsiao Shih, a flute master, and both
drank an elixir and became immortals. It is said that Jade Woman
is washing her hair in a basin because of the five natural rock
mortars—used by hermits to grind grain—that lie directly in
front of a shrine King Mu built on the summit in dedication to
his daughter.

Farewell to Scholar Keng, p. 80

For *Keng's* title, Chia Tao uses the term *ch'u-shih,* which can
mean a retired scholar, a scholar who has not yet embarked on
an official career, or a recluse. The term also connotes a scholar
of exceptional talent and virtue.

*In Early Autumn, Sent to Ling-yin Temple on T'ien-chu Mountain,
for Posting, p. 81*

Ling-yin Temple, founded in 326, is located beyond the west shore
of Hang-chou's West Lake in Chekiang Province. *Mount Wo-
chou* is also in Chekiang Province. *Master Hsieh* (Hsieh-kung) is
Hsieh Ling-yun (385–443), the great lyric poet of the Six Dynas-
ties period. Known as the father of Chinese landscape poetry, he
was also a lay Buddhist and an accomplished painter.

Sending Off T'ang Huan, Returning to a Village on the Fu River, p. 82
The *Fu River* is in present-day western Hua-yun County in Shensi Province. *Mao-nu (Down-Haired Maiden) Peak* is named for a woman who cultivated the Tao. Porter tells her story in *Road to Heaven:*

> Her original name was Yu-chiang, and she once lived in a cave near the summit. When the First Emperor of the Ch'in dynasty died in 210 B.C., a number of his concubines were chosen to join him in eternal repose. Yu-chiang was among those selected to play the heavenly zither. But the night before she was to be taken to the emperor's mausoleum near Lishan, an old eunuch helped her escape to Haushan. Later she met a Taoist master who taught her how to survive on a diet of pine needles and spring water, how to visualize the seven stars of the Big Dipper that connect a person's life force, and how to walk the shaman's Walk of Yu. Through such cultivation, her body became covered with long green hair, and the people started calling her Mao-nu....

The first stanza of the poem suggests that when T'ang Huan returns to the Fu River, he will not only enjoy a fine view of Mao-nu Peak, but also sleep soundly.

For Monk Hung-ch'uan, p. 83
Indigo Mountain is possibly Lan-t'ien Mountain. *Jade wood (yu-lin):* beautiful wood. *Mount T'ai-po* is in southeast Mei County, Shensi Province, about one hundred miles west of Sian.

Winter Moon, Rain in Ch'ang-an, Watching the Chung-nan Mountains in Snow, p. 84
Autumn Festival (Ch'iu-chieh) refers to either Moon Festival or Double Nine (the Mountain Climbing Festival). Since it comes later in the year, I suspect this reference is to Double Nine. On

the other hand, *ch'iu-chieh* could mean autumn of the solar calendar, with the first day of winter *(li-tung)* arriving in early November. The *Pa and Ch'an Rivers* are in the vicinity of Ch'ang-an. The *Hsiao and Hsiang Rivers* are far to the south, in Hunan Province.

Parting from a Friend Entering Shu, p. 86

The ancient kingdom of *Shu* indicates Szechuan Province. *Cho Wen-chun* (fl. 150–115 B.C.), a native of Szechuan, was China's first acclaimed woman poet. *Yang Hsiung* (55 B.C.–18 A.D.), an important philosopher and poet-writer, was a native of Ch'eng-tu, the provincial capital of Shu. The *Min* is a major river in Szechuan that flows through Ch'eng-tu and joins the Yangtze River at Sui-fu. It was once thought to be the headwaters of the Yangtze.

Farewell to Monk Ho-lan, p. 87

A *cloud* can mean a monk.

Overnight at Monk Yun's Room, p. 88

Dots of red ink inserted in a text or commentary served roughly the same purpose as underlining in a modern text. *Grass writing (ts'ao-shu)* is cursive calligraphy.

Sent to Mo-kung on Pai-ko Peak, p. 89

White Pavilion Peak (Pai-ko) is south of Ch'ang-an and close to *Purple Pavilion Peak (Tzu-ko)* and *Yellow Pavilion Peak (Huang-ko)*. See the poem "East Heights Residence, Happy for the Frequent Visits of T'ang Wen-ch'i" (p. 66).

Seeing Off the Mountain Monk Ch'u, Returning to Japan, p. 90

For a detailed account of a Japanese monk's pilgrimage to Buddhist China in 838–847, see *Ennin's Diary: The Record of a Pilgrimage to China in Search of the Law,* translated by Edwin O. Reischauer. This work describes the Buddhist world in the

T'ang Dynasty, as it was near the end of Chia Tao's life. *Eastern Sea:* or Sea of Japan.

Thinking of a Friend Traveling to the Border, p. 91
North of the Yuan River: or beyond the border of northern Kan-su Province. *Red dust (hung-ch'en)* is a Buddhist term referring to the world of the senses. Outside of a Buddhist context, it can mean "the mundane world."

Seeing Off a Friend Traveling to Yueh, p. 92
Yueh was an ancient state occupying the present-day provinces of Fukien and Chekiang. The *eight-line, new-style poems* are the regulated *lu-shih*—the form in which this poem was written.

At Ch'ung-sheng Temple, Pin-kung's Room, p. 93
Ch'ung-sheng Temple was located in Ch'ung-te Ward in south Ch'ang-an. *Nan-yueh,* also known as Heng Mountain, is a sacred mountain located in Hunan Province. *Walking meditation (ching-hsing)* is *kinhin* in Japanese—and now "kinhin" in English. The last line in the Chinese text literally reads: "walking meditation is *hsi-chi,*" the practice of eliminating thoughts of fame and wealth. *Little mind,* in Zen terminology, is the ego-driven mind.

Rainy Night, Sent to Ma Tai, p. 94
Serpentine Lake (Ch'u-chiang) was an artificial lake built in southeast Ch'ang-an for Emperor Wu-ti in the first century B.C. See the poem "East Heights Residence, Happy for the Frequent Visits of T'ang Wen-ch'i" (p. 66). *Ma Tai* was an official and a poet-friend of Chia Tao's. See the poem "At the Hua-shan Hermitage of Adept Ma Tai" (p. 79).

Farewell to a T'ien-t'ai Monk, p. 95
Yueh-yang Stream is in Szechuan near Ch'ang-chiang, where Chia Tao, in exile, served as Registrar late in his life.

Rainy Night with Li Hsuan, Recalling Huang Fu-hsun, p. 96
The setting for this poem is the capital, Ch'ang-an.

Evening Gathering at the Residence of Yao Ho;
K'o-kung Does Not Arrive, p. 97
Yao Ho and the *Hall of Government Affairs:* see the notes to the
poem "Responding to Secretary Yao Ho" (p. 122). *K'o-kung:* see
the notes to the poem "Visiting with Buddhist Monk Wu-k'o
at His Remote Dwelling" (p. 120). The *winter sacrifice* occurs at
the end of the lunar year. *West Spring* is presumably in the direc-
tion of the temple (and stone chimes) at which Monk K'o-kung
was staying in Ch'ang-an.

Sent to Secretary Ch'ang Wu-chu, p. 98
Secretary Ch'ang is not identified, but he is referred to in the Chi-
nese text as a "white robe" *(pai-i)*—a statesman and sage, prob-
ably retired, but retaining great influence. In my translation I refer
to him as *wise sir.* Toward the end of Chia Tao's life, China was at
war with the Uighurs, a nomadic people to the northwest.

Farewell to a Military Enlistee, on the Road, p. 99
The *River I* flows past *Dragon Gate* at a point some thirteen miles
south of the T'ang Dynasty summer capital of Lo-yang. *Sung-
shan,* a mountain south of Lo-yang in Honan Province, is the
central and highest of China's five sacred mountains. *Kuang-ling,*
a site on Serpentine Lake *(Ch'u-chiang),* is famous for the height
of its waves.

Seeing Off Buddhist Master Hsia-yun of T'se-en Temple to an
Audience with Minister of Public Works Li, at T'ai-yuan,
Capital of Shansi, p. 100
T'se-en Temple was located in Ch'ang-an. The city of *T'ai-yuan,*
a military staging area at the time, is located one hundred miles
south of the Great Wall in Shansi Province.

Overnight at Ch'ing-yeh Temple with Li K'uo,
Former Hu District Sub-Prefect Li K'uo, p. 101

See notes to "Response to Sub-Prefect Li K'uo of Hu County"
(p. 116).

For Li of Chin-chou, p. 102

Li of Chin-chou, or Li Cheng-ts'u, was a government official and
friend of Chia Tao. He was demoted to a provincial governor's
post in Chin-chou, located in An-k'ang County, Shensi Province.
Ch'i Li, according to the *Shih-chi (Records of the Grand Histori-
an),* was one of the Four Worthies, a group of men who, during
the Ch'in Dynasty, ventured into the deep mountains southeast
of Ch'ang-an to remain until a more virtuous government came
to power. The *Han River's* source lies not far from the Four Wor-
thies' retreat in southern Shensi Province. It then flows eastward
through Hupei Province, meeting the Yangtze River at Hankow.

Travel Stop on the Han River, p. 103

The Han River. See notes to the preceding poem. *Hsi-chia's* ponds
and lowlands are located in today's Hsiang-yang County in
Hupei Province. *Liu Pei* was a Han Dynasty prince who became
emperor of the state of Shu Han in 221, during the Three King-
doms period. Although his effort to restore the Han Dynasty
failed, his heroic martial exploits are described in the historical-
ly based novel *Romance of the Three Kingdoms.* *The River Hsiang*
is in present-day Hunan Province.

Seeing Off Ch'an Master Hui-ya Returning to Jade Springs, p. 104

Master Hui-ya is unidentified. *Jade Springs* is a mountain in present-
day Tang-yang County in Hupei Province. Jade Springs Temple
is at the foot of the mountain. Both mountain and temple are
within the old borders of the state of Ch'u, a large and power-
ful state that existed 740–223 B.C. See the notes to the poem
"Winter Night Farewell" (p. 111). *The Hsiao and Hsiang Rivers*
are in Hunan Province. *Tung-t'ing Lake* is a large body of water

in northern Hunan, just south of the Yangtze River. *The gorges* are those of the middle Yangtze River. See notes to the poem "Seeing Off Sub-Prefect Mu to Mei-chou" (p. 114). The *chanted verses* are *gathas:* originally verses that capped or summarized sutras, consisting of four three-, five-, or seven-syllable lines. Later, in China, *gathas* became original Buddhist poems in their own right.

Overnight Stay with K'o-kung, p. 106

K'o-kung, or Wu-k'o. *Ts'ao-t'ang* ("humble cottage"; used by hermits) is the name of a temple just below Mount Kuei-feng in today's Shensi Province. *Enlightened Prince* is a euphemism for "emperor."

Farewell to Monk Wu-k'o, p. 107

Wu-k'o, or K'o-kung. A *fly-whisk* was a prop and symbol of Ch'an masters at the time. It was used to add emphasis to ideas and instructional remarks made to practicing monks. It was also a symbol of compassion because when used against insects, it could drive them away without killing them. *T'ien-t'ai* is a mountain in a range of the same name in Chekiang Province. It was the home of the famous T'ang hermit-poet Han-shan. The third stanza (a couplet in the original Chinese) is famous in part because of Chia Tao's poem about writing it:

UPON FINISHING A POEM

It took three years
to get two lines right;

I test them aloud and
my eyes blur with tears.

If for you, friend,
the poem doesn't ring true,

I'll leave off and go back
to the old autumn mountains.

Bibliography

Editions of Chia Tao's Poetry Consulted

Ch'ang-chiang chi. Ssu-pu pei-yao. Shanghai: Chung-hua shu-chu, 1927–1937; reprint, Taipei: China Book Company, 1966.

Ch'en, Yen-chieh, annotator, and Wang Yun-wu, ed. *Chia Tao shih-chu.* Shanghai: Shang-wu yin-shu-kuan, 1937.

Hsu Sung-po, ed. *Lu sheng-chih chi, Ch'ang-chiang chi ho-t'ing-pen.* Taipei: Hsinan Book Co., 1973.

P'eng Ting-ch'iu (1645–1719), ed. *Ch'uan-T'ang-shih.* Taipei: Hungyeh Book Company, 1982.

Translations in English

Liu, Wu-chi, and Irving Yu-cheng Lo, eds. *Sunflower Splendor: Three Thousand Years of Chinese Poetry.* Garden City, N.Y.: Anchor Press/Doubleday, 1975.

O'Connor, Mike. *One with the Snowy Night: Selected Poems of Chia Tao.* Berkeley: Tangram, 1999.

———. *When I Find You Again, It Will Be in Mountains: Selected Poems of Chia Tao.* Berkeley: Tangram, 1996.

———. *Colors of Daybreak and Dust: A Selection of Poems by Chia Tao.* Berkeley: Tangram, 1995.

Owen, Stephen. "Some Mid-T'ang Quatrains." In *A Brotherhood of Song:*

Chinese Poetry and Poetics. Ed. Stephen C. Soong. Hong Kong: Chinese University Press, 1985.

Seaton, J. P., and Dennis Maloney. *A Drifting Boat.* Fredonia, N.Y.: White Pine Press, 1994.

Watson, Burton. "Buddhist Poet-Priests of the T'ang." In *The Eastern Buddhist* 25.2 (1992): 30–58.

Witzling, Catherine (see Studies below).

Note: Owing in part to its inclusion in the *T'ang-shih san-pai shou (Complete Poems of the T'ang),* Chia Tao's "Seeking but Not Finding the Recluse" has been translated numerous times.

STUDIES

Chang, Yu-ming. *Ch'ang-chiang chi chiao-chu.* Master's thesis, Kuo-li Shih-fan Ta-hsueh, Taipei, 1969.

Li, Chia-yen. *Chia Tao nien-p'u.* Peking: 1946; reprint, Taipei: Ta-hsi-yang t'u-shu kung-ssu, 1974.

Liu, Ssu-han, ed. *Meng Chao Chia Tao shih-hsuan.* Taipei: Yuanliu Publishing Co., 1988.

Witzling, Catherine. "The Poetry of Chia Tao: A Re-Examination of Critical Stereotypes." Ph.D. dissertation, Stanford University, 1980.

TOOLS & SELECTED REFERENCES

Bary, Wm. Theodore de, ed. *Sources of Chinese Tradition.* New York: Columbia University Press, 1960.

Blofeld, John, trans. *The Zen Teaching of Huang Po.* New York: Grove Press, 1959.

Bynner, Witter, and Kiang Kang-hu. *The Jade Mountain.* New York: Knopf, 1929; reprint, New York: Doubleday Anchor Book, 1964.

Ch'en, Kenneth. *Buddhism in China*. Princeton, N.J.: Princeton University Press, 1964.

Chinese-English Dictionary of Modern Usage. Lin Yutang. Hong Kong: The Chinese University of Hong Kong, 1972.

Cleary, Thomas. *Entry into the Inconceivable: An Introduction to Hua-Yen Buddhism*. Honolulu: University of Hawai'i Press, 1995.

—————. *The Flower Ornament Scripture: A Translation of the Avatamsaka Sutra*. Boston: Shambhala Publications, 1983.

Conze, Edward. *Buddhist Wisdom Books*. London: George Allen and Unwin, 1958; reprint, London: Harper Torchbooks, 1972.

A Dictionary of Chinese Buddhist Terms. Comp. William Edward Soothill and Lewis Hodus. London: Kegan Paul, Trench, Trubner & Co., 1934; reprint, Taipei: Ch'eng Wen Publishing Co., 1975.

Dumoulin, Heinrich. *Zen Buddhism: A History*. Vol. 1, *India and China*. Trans. James W. Heisig and Paul Knitter. New York: Macmillan Publishing Company; and London: Collier Macmillan Publishers, 1988.

The Encyclopedic Dictionary of the Chinese Language. Ed. Chang Ch'i-yun. Taipei: Chinese Culture University, 1973.

Foster, Nelson, and Jack Shoemaker, eds. *The Roaring Stream: A New Zen Reader*. Hopewell, N.J.: The Ecco Press, 1996.

Graham, A. C. *Poems of the Late T'ang*. Baltimore: Penguin, 1965.

Hansen, Paul, trans. *Before Ten Thousand Peaks*. Port Townsend: Copper Canyon Press, 1980.

Hawkes, David, trans. *Ch'u Tz'u (The Songs of the South)*. Oxford: Oxford University Press, 1959.

Herdan, Innes, trans. *300 T'ang Poems*. Taipei: The Far East Book Co., 1973.

Hinton, David, trans. *The Late Poems of Meng Chiao*. Princeton, N.J.: Princeton University Press, 1996.

Legge, James. *The Chinese Classics: Confucian Analects, The Great Learning, The Doctrine of the Mean and The Works of Mencius*. London: Trubner & Co., 1867–76. Various reprints.

———. *The Chinese Classics*. Vol. 4, *The She King*. Reprint, Taipei: Southern Materials Center, Inc., 1985.

———. *The Sacred Books of China*. London: Oxford University Press, 1891; reprint, New York: Dover Publications, 1962.

Liu, James J.Y. *The Art of Chinese Poetry*. Chicago: University of Chicago Press, 1962.

Lo Kuan-chung. *Three Kingdoms*. Trans. and ed. Moss Roberts. New York: Pantheon Books (Random House), 1976.

Luk, Charles, trans. *The Vimalakirti Nirdesa Sutra*. Berkeley: Shambhala, 1972.

———. *Ch'an and Zen Teaching*. Vol. 2. York Beach, ME: Samuel Weiser, 1993.

Mathews' Chinese-English Dictionary. Comp. R.H. Mathews. Shanghai: China Inland Mission and Presbyterian Mission Press, 1931.

Naquin, Susan, and Chun-fang Yu, eds. *Pilgrims and Sacred Sites in China*. Berkeley: University of California Press, 1992; reprint, Taipei: SMC Publishing Inc., 1994.

A New Practical Chinese-English Dictionary. Ed. Liang Shih-chiu. Taipei: The Far East Book Co., 1972.

Nienhauser, William H., Jr., ed. and comp. *The Indiana Companion to Chinese Literature*. 2nd ed. Bloomington: Indiana University Press, 1986; Taipei: SMC Publishing Inc., 1986.

Owen, Stephen. *The End of the Chinese "Middle Ages": Essays in Mid-T'ang Literary Culture*. Stanford: Stanford University Press, 1996.

———. *The Great Age of Chinese Poetry: The High T'ang*. New Haven: Yale University Press, 1981.

————. *The Poetry of Meng Chiao and Han Yu*. New York and London: Yale University Press, 1975.

————. *Readings in Chinese Literary Thought*. Harvard-Yenching Institute Monograph Series No. 30: Cambridge, MA: Harvard University Press, 1992.

Peterson, C.A. "Court and Province in Mid- and Late T'ang." In *The Cambridge History of China*, Vol. 3, *Sui and T'ang China,* Part I. Gen. ed. Denis Twichett and John K. Fairbank. Cambridge: Cambridge University Press, 1979.

Porter, Bill [Red Pine]. *Road to Heaven: Encounters with Chinese Hermits*. San Francisco: Mercury House, 1993.

————, trans. *The Collected Songs of Cold Mountain*. Port Townsend: Copper Canyon Press, 1983.

Reischauer, Edwin O., trans. *Ennin's Diary: Record of a Pilgrimage to China in Search of the Law*. New York: The Ronald Press Company, 1955.

Suzuki, Daisetz Teitaro. *Manual of Zen Buddhism*. New York: Grove Press, 1960.

Suzuki, Shunryu. *Zen Mind, Beginner's Mind*. New York and Tokyo: Weatherhill, 1970.

Watson, Burton. *Chinese Lyricism: Shih Poetry from the Second to the Twelfth Century*. New York: Columbia University Press, 1971.

————. *The Zen Teachings of Master Lin-chi*. Boston and London: Shambhala, 1993.

————, trans. *Ssu-ma Ch'ien: Grand Historian of China*. New York: Columbia University Press, 1969.

Wu, John C. H. *The Golden Age of Zen*. Rev. ed. Taipei: United Publishing Center, 1975.

Yampolsky, Philip B., trans. *The Platform Sutra of the Sixth Patriarch*. New York: Columbia University Press, 1967.

Yip, Wai-lim. *Ezra Pound's Cathay*. Princeton, N.J.: Princeton University Press, 1969.

―――, ed. and trans. *Chinese Poetry: Major Modes and Genres*. Berkeley, Los Angeles, London: University of California Press.

Yoshikawa Kojiro. *An Introduction to Sung Poetry*. Trans. Burton Watson. Cambridge, M.A.: Harvard University Press, 1967.

Yu, Pauline, trans. and comm. *The Poetry of Wang Wei*. Bloomington: Indiana University Press, 1980.

Yung Liu. *T'ang-shih chu-tien (A Handbook and Index of Chinese T'ang Poetry)*. Taipei: Shui-Yun-Chai Studio, 1986.

Zurcher, E. *The Buddhist Conquest of China*. Leiden, Holland: E.J. Brill, 1959.

Illustrations
by Steven R. Johnson

Biographical Notes

MIKE O'CONNOR, a native of the Olympic Peninsula, Washington, is a poet and translator of Chinese literature. His first formal classes in poetry were under Elizabeth Bishop at the University of Washington. Later, he spent more than a decade farming in the Dungeness River Valley, and cedar logging and tree planting in the Olympic Mountains. In 1979 he traveled to Taiwan, the Republic of China, where he lived for some fourteen years. There he studied Chinese culture and language while working as an editor for *The China Economic News*. He also served as an editor for the quasi-governmental China External Trade and Development Council (CETRA), Taipei. In 1995 he returned to the U.S. and now resides with his wife, Liu Ling-hui, in Port Townsend, Washington. He holds an M.F.A. degree in writing and poetics from the Naropa Institute in Boulder, Colorado, and a B.A. from the Evergreen State College, Olympia, Washington.

His principal books of poetry include *The Basin: Life in a Chinese Province* and *The Rainshadow,* concerning backcountry life on the Olympic Peninsula. His primary works of translation include *Setting Out,* a novel by Taiwanese writer Tung Nien; *The Tienanmen Square Poems;* and, for *Mudlark,* an electronic journal of poetry and poetics, *Only a Friend Can Know*—a mix of original poems and translations on the Chinese theme of *chih-yin* [www.unf.edu/mudlark]. He was also co-editor and a translator of *The Clouds Should Know Me by Now: Buddhist Poet Monks of China.*

STEVEN R. JOHNSON has been a Northwest photographer and painter since 1967. Much of his photography—mostly in black and white—has been inspired by close contact with nature. Since the 1970s his photography has served as a rich resource for environmentalists in their (and his) efforts to protect old-growth forests and wilderness areas of the Olympic Peninsula. In 1984 he collaborated with poet Finn Wilcox on the book *Here Among the Sacrificed,* a powerful visual and poetic documentation of America's hobos riding the rails; and in 1993 he collaborated with writer and translator Bill Porter on *Road to Heaven: Encounters with Chinese Hermits,* a book project that took the photographer to the sacred mountains of China. Currently, Johnson resides in woods near the Straits of Juan de Fuca, not far from Port Townsend, Washington.

Also by Mike O'Connor

THE CLOUDS SHOULD KNOW ME BY NOW

Buddhist Poet Monks of China

Edited by Red Pine and Mike O'Connor

This groundbreaking collection presents the work of fourteen eminent Chinese poet monks, whose works span twelve centuries (700–1900 A.D.). Complete with an historical introduction to each poet, *Clouds* features both the original Chinese and English translations by Burton Watson, J.P. Seaton, Paul Hansen, James Sanford, and the editors.

"Achingly beautiful poems."—*Library Journal*

"Refreshing... These translations will stand alongside those of Pound, Rexroth, Snyder and R.H. Blyth...a valuable addition to collections of Buddhist poetry."—*Choice*

"*Clouds*...could be featured in a display of Zen poetry, Buddhist thought. The Beats revisited, Chinese literature, or even modern poets... The poets consider tangible, ordinary objects in such a way that the objects seems to disappear, almost to dissolve back to their primal state, like clouds hovering over a mountain peak."
—*New Age Retailer*

224 pages, 6 x 9, 0-86171-143-2, $15.95

To order, call 1-800-272-4050, or visit our secure online store at www.wisdompubs.org

ABOUT WISDOM

WISDOM PUBLICATIONS, a not-for-profit publisher, is dedicated to making available authentic Buddhist works by the world's leading Buddhist teachers. We publish our titles with the appreciation of Buddhism as a living philosophy and with the special commitment to preserve and transmit important works from all major Buddhist traditions.

If you would like more information or a copy of our mail-order catalog, please contact us at:

Wisdom Publications
199 Elm Street
Somerville, Massachusetts 02144 USA
Telephone: (617) 776-7416 • Fax: (617) 776-7841
Email: sales@wisdompubs.org • www.wisdompubs.org

THE WISDOM TRUST

As a not-for-profit publisher, Wisdom Publications is dedicated to the publication of fine Dharma books for the benefit of all sentient beings and dependent upon the kindness and generosity of sponsors in order to do so. If you would like to make a donation to Wisdom Publications, please do so through our Somerville office. If you would like to sponsor the publication of a book, please write or email us for more information.

Thank you.

Wisdom Publications is a non-profit, charitable 501(c)(3) organization and a part of the Foundation for the Preservation of the Mahayana Tradition (FPMT).